Beyond the Clash of Civilizations

A New Cultural Synthesis for Muslims in the West

by

Mohamed Wa Baile

iUniverse, Inc.
Bloomington

Beyond the Clash of Civilizations
A New Cultural Synthesis for Muslims in the West

iUniverse books may be ordered through booksellers or by contacting:

iUniverse
1663 Liberty Drive
Bloomington, IN 47403
www.iuniverse.com
1-800-Authors (1-800-288-4677)

Because of the dynamic nature of the Internet, any web addresses or links contained in this book may have changed since publication and may no longer be valid. The views expressed in this work are solely those of the author and do not necessarily reflect the views of the publisher, and the publisher hereby disclaims any responsibility for them.

Any people depicted in stock imagery provided by Thinkstock are models, and such images are being used for illustrative purposes only.

Certain stock imagery © Thinkstock.

ISBN: 978-1-4620-3420-8 (sc)
ISBN: 978-1-4620-3421-5 (e)
ISBN: 978-1-4620-3422-2 (dj)

Library of Congress Control Number: 2011912857

Printed in the United States of America

iUniverse rev. date: 7/29/2011

For my beloved Afropean-Euromuslim daughter, Rahima

Contents

Acknowledgments

While working on my master's thesis, upon which this book is largely based, several families trusted me enough to open their homes so that I could learn about their way of life. Their generosity both touched me and was immensely beneficial. I am deeply grateful to all of them.

I fondly remember many of our discussions, especially with the sons and daughters, whose frankness and honesty extended to difficult, sensitive, and sometimes confusing issues of identity. I would like nothing more than to get together again with these dear friends for more conversation and reflection.

I am forever indebted to my wife. Stephanie has done far more than accompany me along this difficult journey, as inestimable as that has been. She has challenged my thoughts and assumptions about Muslims living in the West and on Islam in general. Stephanie's intelligence has, over the years, been stimulating, to say the least, but she offers it with unstinting love and compassion.

I wish to acknowledge several scholars whose achievements have inspired me from a distance to reflect deeply about the society I live in and to which I seek ways to contribute. I am thinking particularly of Ali Mazrui, Edward W. Said, Johan Galtung, John Esposito, Fatema Mohamed Arkoun, Tariq Ramadan, and Shireen T. Hunter. They have all written important if not seminal works on the question of Islam's relationship with the West, democracy, and modernity. Their output has helped shape not only my thinking, but my way of life.

Finally, the book you are about to read, would not have seen the light of day without my teachers and fellow students. I have learned from them and from the many debates in which I have been privileged to take part. To all I owe a deep debt.

I would like to thank the members of the Swiss Center for Peace Studies, at the World Peace Academy in Basel.

While studying for my master's degree at the Center, I participated in several seminars, worked part time, and took time to be with my lovely daughter. At times it was a harrowing experience from an "organizational" point of view. But that was a unique time for us that will not return. Life is hope. Looking back, the fruits of my labor confirm to me that the experience was worth every minute and every hardship I endured!

To God Almighty belongs the praise. I ask him to give me the strength to "desegregate" the multiple identities I have accumulated along my journey, for I am African, a Muslim, and a Kenyan and Swiss citizen. I am a son, brother, friend, husband, father, and, above all, a human being.

This work does not lay claim to the "right version" of Islam, nor do I pretend to judge what a "right" Muslim should be. All I seek is God's guidance for my own path as a Muslim living and examining his life in the West.

In the name of God the Merciful, the Compassionate.

Praise be to God,
Lord of the Worlds.
The Merciful and Compassionate.
Master of the Day of Judgment.
You alone do we worship,
And from You alone we seek help.

Guide us to the straight path,
The path of those You have blessed,
Not those who are stricken with wrath,
Nor they who are lost.

Amen.

Mohamed Wa Baile
Bern, Switzerland
Summer 2011

Introduction

In the beginning was the Word …

Although we have been speaking words for untold millennia, this scriptural reference has to do with the Word of *God*, the Creator. It signifies the divine truth behind all that which he has created.

Human speech is completely different. It is a natural human faculty. Yet even in this mundane sense, our utterances endow us with a strange kind of power possessed by no other living species on earth. I deliberately use the word *power*.

Power is not only about coercion or the use of brute force to make others behave as we want them to. Even in a context of fierce geopolitical rivalry, "soft diplomacy" can be a powerful tool. And what is soft diplomacy if not persuasion, the success of which ultimately hinges on effective, peaceful dialogue in place of violence?

Words are powerful also because they give us the capacity either to heal or to injure our fellow human beings. We applaud a great speaker for his or her skillful "deployment" of words and the meanings they convey. Words have the power not only to divide us, but to bring us together as human beings, even across seemingly unbridgeable divides.

A good example of the power of words is the historic speech

that United States president Barack Hussein Obama delivered in Cairo, Egypt, on June 4, 2009:

I have come here to seek a new beginning between the United States and Muslims around the world; one based upon mutual interest and mutual respect; and one based upon the truth that America and Islam are not exclusive, and need not be in competition. Instead, they overlap, and share common principles — principles of justice and progress; tolerance and the dignity of all human beings ... There must be a sustained effort to listen to each other; to learn from each other; to respect one another; and to seek common ground.[1]

Echoing inside one of the world's oldest universities, al-Azhar, his words were crafted to convey positive signals about American intentions to more than 1.5 billion concerned Muslims. He reminded his audience of what connected human beings. This is typical of Obama, who is known for the inclusiveness of his political vision.

He knew that the pursuit of peaceful relations was foremost on everyone's mind, his and his audience's, so he focused on relations between Islam and the West and proposed a new and peaceful beginning. He received long and heartfelt applause on that important day, because everyone felt the power of his words. Far from threatening, his language induced people of goodwill everywhere to give him and the nation he represents the benefit of the doubt. As a result, the perception of America began to undergo significant change, at least compared with the period when his predecessor, George W. Bush, had occupied the helm. Since then, this perception has largely eroded, of course,

---

1   Barack Obama, "Text: Obama's Speech in Cairo," *New York Times*, June 4, 2009.

but the fact remains that for a brief moment he succeeded where others have not.

Did he pull it off because of the content of his message? Or was it just his elocution?

Obama's great eloquence had been widely recognized even before his election to office. But there are as many interpretations of his performance as president as there are political views. Back home he is routinely vilified as a "foreign-born terrorist," the "Arab" in the White House Obama, the anti-colonial Mau Mau sympathizer. Or, Obama is bad for America because he is not white enough—or, conversely, not black enough. Despite his being demonized, he has never lost the unifying approach he has been honing for years. He insists on speaking plainly to his fellow Americans about their primary concerns. As battered as they are by the failing economy, many are willing to listen. They too long for national unity, which their country's seemingly intractable problems had shattered.

It is no surprise then that Muslims outside the United States, though living under different conditions, equally understood the unifying thrust of his speech. The ongoing wars in Iraq and Afghanistan, he insisted, should not signify a Christian or American crusade again Islam. They were merely part of America's war on terror. He sent the same message that the United States is not at war against Islam when he announced the killing of Osama bin Laden in May 2011.

Bush used to say the same thing, but somehow it took a man like Obama to persuade enough skeptics to give America another chance. His dialogical approach in the public arena clearly distinguished him from his predecessor. If the polls are correct, Bush scored a positive impact immediately after 9/11, but this rapidly gave way to a consistently negative image both among American voters and abroad. The effect of Obama's language, by contrast, continues to elicit a positive, if rather puzzled, response from large numbers of Americans and those quarters overseas that are still willing to give him the benefit of the doubt.

How words divide and injure

Words are indeed powerful. A mere few pages of Samuel P. Huntington's article "The Clash of Civilizations?" have caused so much ink to be spilled in a full-blown academic debate that it boggles the mind.[2] And then it was one written word in passionate refutation of another. The running debate became so intense that it spilled far beyond academia into soul-searching about foreign policy, immigration, democracy, and so on.

The Satanic Verses is a great example of how the written word can inflame opinion, where language inflicts injury. Salman Rushdie's fiction managed to provoke a radically different response from Huntington's academic-but-specious arguments. It created suspicion, hatred, destruction of property, rioting, and death.

Now, consider *Mein Kampf*. What does this book mean to Jewish people? To Russians? Christians? Atheists? Those who have never read the book?

Given the horrors of the twentieth century, one might think that our loftiest task would be learning to use the power of words to enhance rather than diminish human value or inflame passions with abandon. What is it that makes us human? This is the question we ought to ponder more deeply, exactly the one that has inspired this book.

I will not pretend that the ideas I present here have never been argued before. But it has to be done more purposefully, with more focus, and repeated again and again, because every generation has to learn how to uphold anew the best that lies inside each of us.

---

2   Samuel P. Huntington, "The Clash of Civilizations?" *Foreign Affairs* 72, no. 3 (1993): 22–49, and his book *The Clash of Civilizations and the Remaking of World Order* (London: Free Press, 2002).

The new divides

The past few decades have seen radical changes. True, a fraction of human beings are fabulously wealthy and getting wealthier while whole populations are mired in disease and hunger. The rest of us are somewhere in between. Technology has given this division a wholly new dimension, and there are growing concerns about a "digital divide." If the previous divisions had to do with having or not having enough food, medicine, and so on, the "talk of the town" now is about computer haves and have-nots. This is where the struggle for empowerment is taking shape today.

We are constantly asked to think like a "global village"; we are told there is no other way to understand either the present or the future—with stress on the "future." Poor nations are told that globalization offers them the best hope for gaining some of the prosperity already enjoyed by wealthy states and some "emerging economies." True, globalization—evolving for almost two millennia—has reached a new threshold. We are so interlinked today that we affect each other in ways never before possible. One repercussion of this is that the poor affect the rich as much as the affluent affect those who live on next to nothing. Although overcoming material poverty is clearly still part of the challenge, communications and technology have completely reshaped how we go about it.

Look around you. We have information, products, and services at our disposal, everything at our fingertips. Which products strike your fancy? Here is how you can own this look or self-image right now! Being skinny is no longer a sign of destitution. A thin female body is an object of beauty, unless you happen to prefer the full, buxom look. If this is the image you are pining for, then here is how you too can be "sexy," and these are the products and the information you will need to buy "sexiness"—ANONYMOUSLY. Models are skimpily dressed because they have to match the sensuous ambience of the marketer in the mall, on the Web, or inside the catalogue.

It almost makes no difference what is being advertised. Skinny sells. Half naked sells. If they stopped selling, then some other lure to our base impulses would have to be invented to maintain the all-consuming reality of "choice."

Never mind that those skinny models you see all around throw up their meals just to live up to the body size on which their careers depend. And who defines their careers? Marketers again, of course—for "our" benefit. The same people who impose unlikely criteria for acting and living sexy are telling us that being sexy is within everyone's grasp.

Clearly, not all the developments we have seen, especially in the postwar period, have been healthy. They have led to hyper-consumerism, the depletion of the earth's resources, and climate change. Today, the sheer variety of choices before us, the alternative lifestyles, and the means to their realization is unparalleled. However, the presence of choice on this scale is not a particularly good measure of freedom, which the West purports to uphold. Having to choose between this and that product has no material bearing on the freedom of moral choice or even equality. Purely market driven, it reflects rather a more surreptitious and anonymous kind of socialization. Pervasive materialism has superseded the moral prescriptions we once learned within the family. It foists a new, morally neutral standard of morality upon everyone, the only one deemed worth preserving.

The consequences have been paradoxical. No matter how often Westerners like to say that Western women are equal to men, the reality is far more ambiguous. Some social and cultural trends militate against the ideal of parity between the sexes, reproducing systemic inequalities from the workplace to political institutions. The more women are forced to think and perform like men and the more deeply anonymous socialization reaches into our psyche, the harder it becomes for women to achieve true equality with men.

Interestingly, in other respects, men do not seem to

fare much better than women. Occupying higher positions of responsibility and earning bigger salaries have hardly translated into stress-free lives for men. No longer the sole breadwinners, they are nevertheless psychologically wired for that role. But today, both men and women—parents—have to work hard to make ends meet, and they both have to endure the pressures of the home and the workplace. The old sexual division of labor has all but vanished.

What happens to the children under these conditions?

Simple—just hand them over to day care centers. But the result of this has been that only in the evenings do some families have the chance for meaningful interaction. Even that small time slot has been drastically curtailed by computer games, television, and the Internet. With minimal family interaction, emotional needs go unfilled. There is little quarter left from all the stresses faced in the normal course of life. The result is that personal anxiety can reach crisis proportions in good times as well as bad.

Now, here is the real challenge. How is a modicum of spiritual health possible under these circumstances? I do not mean spiritual in just the religious sense. Spirituality is much more than a set of beliefs and rituals. The moral awareness of *anything* beyond the materially cluttered world we live in may count as "spiritual."

Tragically, when spiritual awareness runs counter to the general trend, millions of spiritually thirsty men, women, and children risk having their choices belittled or, worse, put on trial and banished. Why? Because another segment of the population, somewhat harder to define, happens to regard spirituality in any form as irrational. Why discuss spirituality or religion when science has supposedly replaced both? It is backward and intolerable in a "modern society."

In a secularized world, those who devote themselves to religion are expected to submit to values narrowly defined by the *absence* of religion, rather than the *presence* of anything else in particular. Instead of religion, we have a coterie of reigning ideologies, whose only common denominator is the absence of organized religion. Homosexuality, premarital sex, pornography, consumption, bearing children out of wedlock—they all constitute the telltale signs of progress. The trouble is that none is tolerable or can be incorporated into a mainstream system of religious value-prescriptions that is as old as time. It's all new, and yet it is peddled as something natural and too obvious to need justification.

Liberty enlists freedom of choice to subjugate liberty. This is no longer just another paradox, but a perversion, considering the implications.

Many religious people disapprove of abortion on religious grounds, believing that only God should take away life. But this fact irritates atheists and agnostics when it fails to amuse them. Therefore, the critics of abortion must be publicly ridiculed and humiliated. Never mind that some people, while professing no allegiance to organized religion, share some of the values held by religious people.

I am not advocating for any particular stance on any issue in this book. My point is that the modern lifestyle has created new social divides, and each side considers the other either lost or irrational. Suppressing the other side "because this is the way they are" spells loss of freedom. We are drowning in the infinite number of computer games, perfumes, and brands of tissue paper we "need" to buy, but that is all right. Only the public practice of religion is out of bounds.

However, spiritual and moral issues cannot be wished away. Reflecting upon them, embracing some, and rejecting others—it is all part of what makes us human. In fact, reflecting beyond the material world makes up the most important part. It is what I call, in the broadest possible sense, man's *spirituality*. Spirituality is a faculty or sensibility—however you want to look at it—that is irrepressible.

No matter how secularized, Westerners have always had

spiritual preoccupations. Spirituality did not suddenly appear under the influence of Muslims living in their midst, nor are Muslims the only citizens who need to express their spirituality. Nonreligious people as well as Christians, Jewish people, and Muslims have a similar need.

I hope my work advances the search for a viable response to issues plaguing Western Muslims, or Muslims residing in the West, and by extension assists other Westerners in their quest for personal fulfillment. We must constantly strive for what is higher in our existence, not just the lowest common denominator.

Is "self-redefinition" part of the answer?

Muslims are often pictured suspiciously as being hostile to "secularism" because they cannot seem to adjust to an attitude of noncommittal tolerance toward everything. This view points up the European understanding of "democracy" based on uniformity. Because Islam, the religion of Muslims itself, is a threat to European outlook, it must be constrained. Europeans have gone so far as to forbid the construction of minarets, as Switzerland has done. Liberty in the service of suppression of rights—how paradoxical! No other religious minority has been denied its rights as much as Muslims.

It must be said, however, that they have not helped much in dispelling the misconceptions. They too look upon others, the wider society, as a threat to their way of life. Only, the symmetry stops there, because—unlike native Europeans— their attitude can only marginalize them further. Let us be frank: some Muslims seem to prefer total marginalization to integration of any kind. They ghetto-ize themselves on the pretext that participation in the broader community signifies "conversion" to it, which is *haram* (forbidden) to them.

There is no denying that living as Muslims in the West has become a burden—though the sentiment is hardly unique to Muslims. Having witnessed the callous, intolerant, and antidemocratic banning of minarets on mosques—not to mention the tired, mind-numbing litany of protests against the wearing of the veil—I have the sense that we all need to step back. I hope my focus on helping Muslims put their house in order can contribute to a better society for all.

So, let us start with the Islamic community. To this end, I want to pose a question that has troubled me for quite some time. Have Muslims properly *defined* themselves in their European surroundings? I am referring both to Muslims who are from other continents and have found a new home in Western Europe and also to Muslims who are indigenous to Europe.

I realize that redefining itself is one of the hardest things for any community to do. The reason for this is obvious: people normally have little need to do it, consciously and deliberately, so long as they live in their ancestral homeland and there is no pressure. The trouble arises when they migrate to other lands and inertia or the propensity to continue living as they always had remains strong. Many Muslims in Western Europe and the United States feel more comfortable living as they did back home in Somalia, Yemen, or Bosnia. Even Swiss Muslims (both converts and second- or third-generation children of immigrants) tend to live in the manner they have learned from non-native Muslims. It is as if they were not Swiss at all.

Another tendency is for Muslims of different ethnic backgrounds to gravitate toward a version of Islam that is practiced by people whose language happens to be Arabic. They tend to mistake Arab culture—as varied as it is—for Islam. I think this kind of blunder falls in the same category of well-known scholars such as Samuel Huntington, who wrongly assumes that Muslim equals Arab. Never mind that there are about 20 million Christian Arabs, or that the Arab world in all its astounding variety represents a small percentage of the world's Muslim population.

This is elementary, but confronting head-on the

misconception by which Islam is identified with *any* ethnicity at all may open the door to a fuller Muslim life right here in the West. Short of this, I am certain that Muslims are fated to continue suffering an identity crisis that their parents have unwittingly complicated with their faulty or incomplete understanding of Islam. Islamic upbringing is not about dry rigidity. I personally know daughters who have been cast away by their families because they refused to cover their bodies "enough" (a sign of disobedience to Islam). Some have moved out before being chased away. They simply could not swallow their parents' version of Islam, which appeared too distant from the cultural context in which they lived day in and day out.

If these families are to avoid tearing themselves apart, they need to take stock of their place and time. Central to their concerns is how to be both Muslim and Swiss. Indeed, how does one become a *European* Muslim, *tout court*? This is the perennial question that I and thousands of my generation now, more than ever, must endeavor seriously to answer. That is precisely what this book seeks to explore.

Method of study

This work does not hinge on the findings of surveys, polls, or any other quantitative gathering of data. Instead, it seeks new meanings and alternative ways of thinking for use in the ongoing debate among and about Muslims. I have availed myself, first, of the existing literature on issues that Muslims face in the West. There is a growing body of information also in the Swiss press and television.

I have also conducted interviews with three Muslim community leaders and Muslims from different communities in Bern. These interviews were more or less unstructured, and I have kept the names of all the interviewees anonymous. They focused mostly on the issues plaguing Muslims and possible solutions that could stabilize the situation and lead to peaceful coexistence.

As a practicing Muslim, I am privileged to have unconditional access to various Muslim communities for direct observation. My contacts include people in Austria, Germany, Holland, the United Kingdom, and, most important, Switzerland. For a decade, I have observed Bern's and Basel's Muslim communities particularly closely, examining how individuals, parents, their children, males, females, young, and old interact in the light of the specific conditions under which they live. My observations stretch back to the year 2000 and cover many nationalities, ethnicities, and *madhahib* (Muslim schools of thought). Besides the congregational prayers and *khutbahs* (sermons) I have regularly attended, mostly in the *Islamische Zentrum* Bern (Islamic Center of Bern), I sat with *tablighi jamaat* (society for spreading Islamic faith) for young and old alike, and have joined *tarawehs* and *tahajjuds* prayers during the months of Ramadan.

This work is part of the new beginning we all hope is under way in the community, a long process of understanding and assessment of the real challenges confronting us in the West.

PART I:
Clash or Domination?

- 1 -
Who Are the Muslims of Switzerland?

THE FIRST LARGE WAVE of Muslim migration into Switzerland, Germany, and other West European countries began in the early years of the post-World War II period with predominantly Yugoslav and Turkish *Gastarbeiter* (guest workers). This is no longer the case. Today Muslims from around the world take up residence in Switzerland and other Western European countries for a variety of reasons.

Numbering around 400,000, Muslims make up a significant, if diverse, part of modern Switzerland. Some mosques attract worshippers of close to a hundred different nationalities. A Bedouin Yemenite will pray next to a Yoruba Nigerian; the next line finds a Swahili-speaker from Kenya standing shoulder to shoulder with a Turkish Kurd, Malay, Saudi, Chechnyan, Swiss, or an American. And on top of their national origin, significant ethno-cultural differences separate them, not to mention differing affiliations based on the *madhhab* (religious tradition).

Muslims have generally come to accept an unfamiliar reality, to which they have had to adjust, where their fellow Muslims act and even pray differently from them. As accustomed as they have grown to differences inside the mosque, however, they have met with hostility from the outside because collectively they are distinct from it. This hostility has crystallized into a surge of public opinion favoring the ban on minaret construction (approved by 57.5 percent of Swiss voters in a November 2009 referendum), and may lead to a ban on headscarves in schools and face veils inside public institutions.

This atmosphere has profited the Schweizerische Volkspartei (SVP, or Swiss People's Party). In a spirit of *corps d'élite*, many Swiss politicians have taken it upon themselves to denounce the "Islamization" of Switzerland, accusing Muslims of harboring a dangerous desire to apply and enforce the Shari'ah.

Does crisis of intolerance prove the "clash theory"?

Huntington's thesis of the "clash of civilizations" identifies cultural and religious differences as the primary source of conflict after the fall of Soviet Communism. This view became a compelling narrative after a group of shadowy al-Qaeda terrorists attacked New York's World Trade Center on September 11, 2001. The attack, which has been widely viewed as a vindication of the "clash" theory, no doubt triggered an instance of macro-level clash, which then ramified into a series of micro-, intrastate events in Europe such as the November 2010 ban on the construction of minarets. The advocates of Huntington's thesis inferred from this that Islam must be incompatible with Western life.

Although religion, as a belief system, is only one aspect of civilization, Huntington takes it as the main active component of collective identity. Following his logic, the social problems besetting immigrant communities—criminality, domestic violence, and unemployment—begin to look like problems rooted in religion. They have, in effect, become "Islamized," thereby conflating terrorist acts (themselves committed for a variety of reasons) with the problems of honor killings and genital mutilation.

What does it matter which part of the world any of these abominations happen to originate from? Islam is the common thread, and it is Islam that has to be dealt with through strict legal measures and law enforcement. After all, this is a question of security.

My thesis: From victims to victors

Huntington's thesis propounds a lopsided view of the world and of Islam that will not stand the test of time. Muslims are now a permanent part of Swiss society, and no amount of collective self-exculpation for the ills created by long decades of misguided domestic policies will change that. But rather than succumb to the core assumptions of this view, Muslims have to change their outlook from that of victims of conflict to the victors of peace.

The best way to achieve this, however, is by practicing their religion properly attuned to its time and social context. Practicing Islam in a Swiss-European context and behaving like Swiss-European Muslims are not pipe dreams. There is precedent. Islam has been "Western" nearly as long as Christianity has been "Eastern."

Many reform-minded Muslims have tried to work out an Islamic framework for the Western context in which they live. Based on my studies of their works, I demonstrate to Switzerland's Muslims how to be Helvetia Muslims. Not unlike Christians and followers of most other religions, Muslims exhibit a broad diversity of practices and interpretations of their faith. Islam has a tremendous capacity for adaptation to new settings—it has acquired an Asian face as readily as it did an African or Arab one. Why not a Western face?

In Western Europe and North America, Muslims are equally capable as Asians and Africans of shaping their practices and interpretations for their particular conditions. Indeed it is already happening. Young people have wasted no time in redefining their identity. Nothing in Islam prevents them

5

from doing this. Combining Islamic and ethnic values with elements from the host culture is both positive and permitted by the highest traditions of Islamic jurisprudence. Given this openness to change, Switzerland's Muslims should have no trouble identifying with the core values enshrined in the Swiss Federal Constitution.

I admit that their internal debate on alternative directions has taken place largely within academia, whereas a practical solution has to engage all of Europe's Muslims. Everyone, not just the intellectual leaders of reform, has to explore the possibilities of peaceful coexistence in their new homelands. But the most enduring "peace" comes from self-understanding, which requires more creative ways to explore. The question is how the experiences of Muslims from every walk of life can contribute to and enrich the community as a whole.

A crucial step in this direction is, on the one hand, for Swiss society to tear down the walls preventing greater and more wide-ranging participation in Swiss society. On the other, Muslims collectively have to dissociate themselves from the psychology of victimhood. The way forward is to practice Islam within the Swiss context; playing the victims will not get them there.

This is hardly a radical idea. Indian Muslims are Asian, but not Arab. African Muslims live in an African, not Asian, environment. They do not need to assimilate into Arab culture, and they remain Muslims in the fullest sense of the word. Muslims from different regions in Africa, Asia, and Eastern Europe display patterns where aspects of their cultures are integrated with Islam. Muslims of Western Europe have to reach what is, in my mind, the point of collective maturity where they can say with equal conviction that they are Muslim *and* Swiss or French, British or German, and so on. Perhaps their diverse origins, coming as they do from a host of other countries and regions, would need a long time frame to adopt Islam within their contemporary Western world.

My view is that the harder they persevere on the path of reform, the sooner they will be true masters of their destiny, ultimately to be counted among the *victors of social peace,* regardless of the present obstacles.

Fear of reform

Many ordinary Muslims living in the West have not yet fully internalized the idea of internal reform. To them the intellectual pioneers of Islamic reform are too freewheeling with matters of religion. However, this attitude may have less to do with the idea of reform than with a preference for religious teachers, people with recognized authority, to lay down religious legal opinions and rulings for all to abide by. The assumption is that too much intellectualism spoils the faith.

Although it is not very Islamic to think uncritically, an overreliance on authority has led to widespread inertia. Ordinary folks already have a tough time ordering their daily lives in alien environments, so it is hardly surprising that they should be drawn first to ready-made, accessible formulas for conduct that need no further debate.[3] Muslim intellectuals have failed them because they "do not meet the demands of the religious market."[4] Their ideas are overwrought and too sophisticated to strike a chord in the community at large.

The result is that Muslims generally know little about alternative currents of thought, and because they lack knowledge, they seek solutions based on the culture and customs they know best. Unfortunately, the solutions that may have worked in the "old country" will not necessarily take them far in their new life in Europe. To remedy this, reformists—in the most general, nonpolitical sense—should begin by not coming off as the proponents of stances that seem

3   Olivier Roy, *Globalised Islam: The Search of a New Ummah* (London: Hurst, 2004), 30–31.
4   Ibid.

7

abhorrent to general Muslim sentiment, let alone a fifteen-centuries-old, world-changing Islamic tradition.

The stuff of adaptation

I think this state of affairs has deprived the community of a rich and authentic voice. The choice we are left with is either to pick up where the intellectuals have failed or to fall back on blind imitation.

I have identified the most authentic Islamic sources that I believe will be crucial to genuine reform in the future but that religious scholars who should know better too easily dismiss. My arguments in this book hinge on the Islamic legal concept of *'urf* (custom). Integrating 'urf has enabled Muslims throughout history to adapt in orderly fashion to every cultural, legal, and even normative environment they have encountered. Islam flowered as the greatest, most brilliant civilization the world had ever seen, in part because of its "religious pragmatism," if I could call it that.

Strangely enough, many reformists have shied away from an approach based on custom, in the words of Ahmad Atif Ahmad, "out of fear that an argument from common customs would be dismissed out of hand, or out of fear that social custom will not support their reform projects."[5] Ahmad counters that "Muslim societies can adapt themselves to Western cultural and legal norms, but these norms will, in due time, become Muslim norms and will likely take forms that differ from their Western counterparts."[6] Although he is of the view that Muslims will remain distinctive, how distinctive is a good question. Muslims will continue to differ from each other in various respects—as do Westerners, who are by no means monolithic in political opinion, religion, culture, and so forth. It is simply part of the

---

5   Ahmad Atif Ahmad, *Islam, Modernity, Violence, and Everyday Life* (New York: Palgrave Macmillan, 2009), 115.
6 Ibid.

natural evolution of social groups. Locally shared customs tend to bind people more than their differences.

A few observations

In light of the above, here are six observations to guide the reader through the arguments I present in this book:

1. Conflict may develop because of ideological, social, economical, racial, cultural, or even religious differences. Therefore, religion and culture are only two elements that can create crisis.

2. Conflict occurs not only between civilizations, but also within each civilization. True, Muslims prevail over a huge part of the world, with a population to match, but they also reside in Europe and have been there for numerous centuries. They experience conflicts there themselves as well as with their host Western mores.

3. Reconciling Islamic belief with Western values is the biggest challenge facing Muslims in Europe. They have no choice but to make this process integral to their maturation into *European* Muslims, not just Muslims living in Europe.

4. Unless Muslims in the West redefine their identity within their immediate context, their internal fissures will widen and more conflict will erupt among themselves as well as with non-Muslim neighbors.

5. Interreligious or civilizational dialogue fosters peaceful coexistence between Muslims and non-Muslims. In the West it will be fruitful only if it begins with a separate dialogue aimed at reconciling Muslims' internal differences, and if Muslims can distinguish the core of faith from its external

expression. Culture and contextualization in time and place change; the essence of the faith need not.

6. An Islamic framework that could be applied within a Western context has to rest on the compatibility of two aspects of identity: the Muslim and the local ones. There is nothing inevitable about the clash between being a good Muslim and a good Swiss citizen. This idea—largely academic for now—has not quite reached Switzerland's Muslim community at large.

- 2 -
In the Name of Civilization:
"Islam and the West"

"ISLAM AND THE WEST"—IT used to sound perfectly innocuous. Yet the historical character of this critical axis in international and intercultural relations has been distorted by sheer intellectual dishonesty and mythmaking. Following the Red Menace, the Islamic Threat is the new bogeyman, a Cyclops ready to chomp on the West limb by limb. Clearly, Islam has replaced Communism in the minds of many in the Western intelligentsia and political classes.

Deliberately or not, Harvard professor Samuel P. Huntington has put himself at the center of a new, more horrific vision of endless conflict, that of the "clash of civilizations." His thesis, that cultural and religious differences are the primary source of conflict after the fall of Communism, has provoked a worldwide debate. No less a figure than reform-minded Iranian president Muhammad Khatami responded to it, declaring the following at the UN Roundtable on Dialogue Among Civilizations[7]:

In order to provide natural unity and harmony in form and

---

7   Muhammad Khatami, "Dialogue Among Civilizations," UNESCO: http://www.unesco.org/dialogue/en/khatami.htm, 2000 [accessed May 24, 2010].

content for global culture and to prevent anarchy and chaos, all concerned parties should engage in a dialogue in which they can exchange knowledge, experience and understanding in diverse areas of culture and civilization.[8]

This is a view that needs to be cultivated around the world. But as laudable as it is, I would still like to move away from the focus on Islam as a global civilization, which of course it is, and limit our scope to Islam as a *religious* presence in the West (Europe, North America, Australia, and so on).

This, first and foremost, is the nature of its presence in Western Europe, beyond which lies the separate issue of Islam as a global civilization. Huntington has confused these two distinct perspectives of Islam.

The roots of the confusion

One must ask: Why is a religion pictured to be in conflict because of its geographical presence?

As Andrea Lueg points out, "it is not Islam and Christianity that are contrasted or the West and the East, but Islam and the West, a religion and a geographical area."[9] The comparison is simply incongruous. Bernard Lewis too has noted the asymmetry of using a geographical label for one group but a religious one for the other, adding, "the term Islam is the counterpart not only of 'Christianity' but also of 'Christendom'— not only of a religion in the narrow Western sense, but of a whole civilization which grew up under the aegis of that religion."[10]

8   "Address by H. E. Mr. Mohammed Khatami, President of the Islamic Republic of Iran," *Round Table: Dialogue among Civilizations*, United Nations (New York: September 5, 2000), provisional verbatim transcription. http://www.unesco.org/dialogue/en/khatami.htm [accessed retrieved February 1, 2011].
9   J. Hippler and A. Lueg, eds., "The Perceptions of Islam in Western Debate," *The Next Threat*, transl L. Friese (London: Pluto Press, 1995), 21.
10   Bernard Lewis, *Islam and the West* (New York: Oxford University Press, 1993), 4.

The language and reasoning behind the "miscomparison" have their roots in the Cold War period, which created what Hippler and Lueg call the "necessary enemy."

> We no longer have the Soviet Union or Communism to serve as enemies justifying expensive and extensive military apparatus. It was in the mid-1980s at the very latest that the search began for new enemies to justify arms budgets and offensive military policies, at first as part of the Communist threat and then in its place.[11]

Huntington tries to make sense of predictions for the post–Cold War period by identifying Islam as the new enemy of the West that replaces the old, an identification that infected the thinking of other intellectuals, such as Francis Fukuyama.[12] Others, like Fred Halliday, have sought to refute the notion that there should be such a thing as a "necessary enemy." "Western society as a whole and Western capitalism in particular," he said, "has never 'needed' an enemy in some systemic sense."[13]

Although Huntington popularized the idea of the "clash of civilizations," it was actually Bernard Lewis who coined it. In a 1993 *Atlantic Monthly* article, he wrote as follows:

> It should now be clear that we are facing a mood and a movement far transcending the level of issues and policies and the governments that pursue them. This is no less than a clash of civilizations — perhaps irrational but surely historic reaction of an ancient rival against

11   Hippler and Lueg, "The Perceptions of Islam in Western Debate," 4.
12   Francis Fukayama has written on post–Cold War history, including "The End of History," *The National Interest* (Summer 1989), http://www.wesjones.com/eoh.htm[24.05.2010], 16; and *The End of History and the Last Man* (New York: Free Press, 1992).
13 Fred Halliday, *Islam & the Myth of Confrontation* (New York: I. B. Tauris, 1996), 113.

our Judeo-Christian heritage, our secular present and the worldwide expansion of both. It is crucially important that we on our side should not be provoked into an equally historic but also equally irrational reaction against that rival.[14]

The article failed to provoke the same level of debate that later surrounded Huntington's popularization of Lewis's ideas. But the idea of a global clash, like Huntington's, is based on a view of Islam of which others have made short shrift. Edward Said accused Lewis of picturing Islam as monolithic. Although influenced by the same fallacious line of thinking, Fukuyama, unlike Huntington and Lewis, argues that liberal democratic ideals, now "universal," have opened up generally optimistic prospects for harmonious relations in the international order. He summarizes his view of this order as follows:

What we may be witnessing is not just the end of the Cold War, or the passing of a particular period of post-war history, but the end of history as such: That is, the end point of mankind's ideological evolution and the universalization of Western liberal democracy as the final form of human government.[15]

Therefore, Fukuyama and Huntington agree fundamentally that the Western way—whether because of its democracy or the character of its civilization—is superior to all others. Fukuyama places Western liberal democracy at the peak of human evolution and predicts that ever more countries will adopt it for themselves. Interestingly, Huntington too believes that the age of ideology has ended. In contrast to Fukuyama,

---

14   Bernard Lewis, "The Roots of Muslim Rage," *The Atlantic Monthly* (1990), 266(3). Online version [May 24, 2010].
15   Fukuyuma, *The End of History and the Last Man* (1992), 5.

though, he ridiculed the notion that the global conflict could draw to a close just because "the war of ideas is at an end."[16] To those expecting harmony because the Berlin Wall has come down and Communist regimes have collapsed, he replied, "Halleluja! We study war no more because war is no more."[17]

After the Cold War, he insisted, the new trend will increasingly be toward cultural conflict and civilizational division. His only complaint is that Westerners harbor an arrogant "missionary" zeal they inherited from times of slavery and colonization that continues under the banner of democracy. The promotion of Western values such as liberal democracy and universalism is naïve and will only provoke further civilizational conflicts.[18] He recommends that the West promote unity within its own sphere of civilization, to support those civilizations that are sympathetic to it, and assist the institutions that legitimize Western civilization.[19]

"Civilization" and its discontents

The term *civilization* has been bandied about throughout this debate almost willy-nilly, but what exactly does it mean and to whom?

To Huntington, *civilization* refers to the highest level of cultural identity, and therein lies the principal source of wider conflict.

It is my hypothesis that the fundamental source of conflict in this new world will not be primarily ideological or primarily economic. The great divisions among humankind and the dominating source of conflict will be cultural. Nation states will remain the

---

16   Huntington, *The Clash of Civilizations and the Remaking of World Order* (2002), 31.
17   Ibid., 31.
18   Ibid., 183–98.
19   Huntington, "The Clash of Civilizations?" *Foreign Affairs* 72, no. 3 (1993): 49.

most powerful actors in world affairs, but the principal conflicts of global politics will occur between nations and groups of different civilizations. The clash of civilizations will dominate global politics. The fault lines between civilizations will be the battle lines of the future.[20]

This is how he frames the future of conflict. Neither social class nor other factors can equal the cultural fissures that separate nations and civilizations.[21] Civilization is *the* factor that will propel future conflicts. Before Huntington, political analysts were accustomed to ideological and other determinants, such as economic inequality, underdevelopment, and security.[22] The presence and organic interaction of these factors, which once accounted for the bulk of tensions, have now been completely eclipsed.

Jochen Hippler has taken Huntington to task for his obsession with culture and religion, charging that the "clash of civilizations" hypothesis is "racist."

Huntington's image of Islam (or of other Asian cultures) is hardly original. It follows the current stereotypes and clinches of popular literature and some media ... According to Huntington, it is not the clash of interests that leads to conflict; the simple fact is that differences between cultures engender war. In a certain sense you could call his argument 'culturally racist'. The Muslims (or Chinese) are *different* from us and *therefore* dangerous. Unlike in classic racism, this difference is not genetically but culturally based. There is such a

---

20 Ibid., 22.
21 Huntington, *The Clash of Civilizations and the Remaking of World Order*, 28.
22 Shireen T. Hunter, *The Future of Islam and the West: Clash of Civilizations or Peaceful Coexistence?* (Westport, CT: Praeger, 1998), 7.

gulf between their values and ways of thinking and ours that understanding or cross-pollination is almost unthinkable. Only military solutions can promise results.[23]

In place of cultural or religious differences, Hippler points to national interests and foreign policies as some of the leading causes of conflict. Shireen T. Hunter concurs with this assessment and concludes that "the real cause of conflict between Islam and the West is not civilizational compatibility."[24] She explains that relations between the Western countries and all Muslim states would be hostile if that were the case. And yet predominantly Shi'ite Iran had close relations with the West under the regime of the Pahlavi dynasty; the West profits from intimate relations with Saudi Arabia and Pakistan. Islam lies at the core of people's collective identity in all these nations; it organizes civil society and even inspires the official state ideologies.[25] Hunter quotes Graham Fuller, who asserts, "A civilizational clash is not so much over Jesus Christ, Confucius, or the Prophet Muhammad as it is over the unequal distribution of world power, wealth, and influence."[26] It is a conflict between the mighty and the powerless, the rich and the poor, not what Huntington argues.

This more sober framework goes much further than Huntington in explaining current trends in international relations. Any perceived threat to Western interests is directly proportional to the degree of divergence or challenge it represents to those Western policies that emanate from those interests. Just as the West acts in accordance with its interests,

23 Jochen Hippler, "The Islamic Threat and Western Foreign Policy," in *The next threat: Western perceptions of Islam*, edited by Jochen Hippler and Andrea Lueg; translated by Laila Friese (London: Pluto Press, 1995), p. 148-9.
24 Hunter, *The Future of Islam and the West*, 19.
25 Ibid.
26 Ibid., 21.

so do a variety of Muslim nations. Why should things be any different? And why do we need a theory as grand and sweeping as Huntington's to explain the specific relations that states keep with each other?

And we must further ask, What makes the Saudi ruling family so friendly to Western interests with the radical salafist character of its rule? The idea of Saudi Arabian women driving is roundly frowned upon. How exactly does this fit with Western "interests"? It does because other, more important considerations impinge on our view of the Saudi Kingdom.

The friendship between this Saudi Kingdom as well as other Arab monarchies such as Oman, Jordan and Morocco with the US for example, is well captured by President Obama's silence on 2011 demonstrations and with his statement on his Arab Spring speech that promises to keep "commitments to friends and partners." Friends and partners here are meant to be Tunisian's Ben Ali, Egypt's Mubarak, Yemen's Saleh, Bahrain's Al Khalifa, and the two Abdullahs of Jordan and Saudi Arabia—to mention but a few.

While the popular Arab appraising is crying for democracy, the current US policy is supporting monarchies and dictators to the end. What a hypocrisy for those preaching democracy and above all what a contradiction with the clash of civilizations thesis! A world-renowned scholar Noam Chomsky speaking at the 25th anniversary celebration of the national media watch group Fairness and Accuracy in Reporting, observes that it is the tradition of the U.S. to supports dictators to control the region, and this is why "The U.S. and Its Allies Will Do Anything to Prevent Democracy in the Arab World".[27]

The point is that incompatibility of values has not significantly impaired relations with many, if not most, Muslims countries. The West continues to denounce the rights'

---

27   Noam Chomsky: "The U.S. and Its Allies Will Do Anything to Prevent Democracy in the Arab World" in *Democracy Now!* http://www. democracynow.org/ [accessed May 21, 2011].

violations of undemocratic governments while praising those same governments for overriding strategic reasons. Some say this reflects a double standard.

On this score Huntington is in full agreement.

Non-Westerners also do not hesitate to point to the gaps between Western principle and Western action. Hypocrisy, double standards, and "but not" are the price of universalist pretensions. Democracy is promoted but not if it brings Islamic fundamentalists to power; nonproliferation is preached for Iran and Iraq but not for Israel; free trade is the elixir of economic growth but not for agriculture; human rights are an issue with China but not with Saudi Arabia; aggression against oil-owning Kuwaitis is massively repulsed but not against non-oil-owning Bosnians. Double standards in practice are the unavoidable price of universal standards of principle.[28]

Where indeed does one situate the American intervention in Muslim oil-producing Kuwait against Iraq, another Muslim country? The question becomes complex when we consider that the military forces arrayed against Saddam Hussein—American, British, Saudi, Syrian, and Egyptian—came from two "civilizations." Why should we not interpret this as evidence of Islamic civilization joining hands with the West to fight against Islamic civilization?

International conflicts are too complex to be explained away by Huntington's reductionist theory. To be blunt, cultural differences explain almost nothing about them. The Gulf War was not an instance of clashing cultures or civilizations, but a conflict involving a host of national, economic, political, and

---

28 Huntington, *The Clash of Civilizations and the Remaking of World Order*, 184.

strategic interests. At no stage of the war did Islam challenge the West.

True, Muslim nations are too weak to mount a serious challenge to the West. But the reality is that Muslims also are not a global *ummah* (community in Islam) in any but the most spiritual sense—incidentally, the way it is supposed to be in the first place. They are divided along ethnic, sectarian, and ideological lines.

Then there is the subject of terrorism. Why is terrorism a threat only to the West but not to non-Western societies? The September 11 attack devoured Muslims as well as non-Muslims. Muslims die in droves in terrorist acts against civilians in Pakistan, Algeria, Iran, Afghanistan, and Iraq. No matter how much they disavow indiscriminate violence, they continue to suffer from it. Going by the number of victims alone, terrorism has affected Muslims the most.

In place of Huntington's weak assessment-cum-prognostication, Hunter suggests the following: one, the ideological battles of the twentieth century were, at the very least, just as intra-civilizational as they were inter-civilizational; two, intra-civilizational conflict characterizes the most prevalent type of conflict in the present context of geopolitics.[29]

Comparing apples and oranges

Huntington's understanding of civilization as the broadest level of cultural identity effectively equates culture with civilization. But what exactly is culture?

Hunter uses Clifford Geertz to define culture as "the totality of socially transmitted behavior patterns, art, beliefs, institutions, and all other products of human work and thought characteristic of a community or population."[30]

The theory of a clash of civilizations plays a fast sleight of hand when it attributes behavior in some civilizations to

---

29 Hunter, *The Future of Islam and the West*, 8–11.
30 Hunter, *The Future of Islam and the West*, 8.

religious culture, then claims that the incompatibility of Islam as a *religion* is fundamentally why it is destined to clash with the West. Besides the Western, there are several major civilizations: Sinic, Japanese, Latin American, Islamic, Slavic-Orthodox, Hindu, and lastly, African. Those civilizations that pose the most significant challenge to other civilizations—namely, the West—are the Sinic and Islamic, because their values are supposedly so distinct.

What troubles me about this scheme is how Huntington refers to the Greater Middle East as a religiously based civilization, but not the West. He equally ignores Christian Latin America. He refers to it simply as "Latin American civilization," even though the overwhelming majority is Catholic and Catholicism has shaped its history. And what about Buddhism? Why does he deny it the status of a major civilization? Japan is the only nation-state that he recognizes as a separate civilization. Whereas Japanese culture equals Japanese civilization, however, some countries share two civilizations, according to Huntington's map. Nigeria has a foothold in both the Islamic and African civilizations, India the Islamic and Hindu civilizations.

Galymzhan Kirbassov's comment on Huntington's classification is revealing.

The most interesting problem that occurred in classification was to which civilization Israel belongs. The question is significant, as Israel has had many disputes with its neighboring states. Huntington thinks Israel is an Islamic civilization according to the map. It is ironic that Israel is considered an Islamic civilization, first because it has nothing to do with the religion of Islam, and second because such an approach decreases empirical support for Huntington's argument.

> Although it does not make sense, I classified Israel as Islamic, strictly adhering to the map.[31]

Not only does Huntington delude himself into supposing that Arabs are the same or are all "Muslim" (there are about 20 million Christian Arabs), but he also places Israel in the civilization of Islam. Which part of Russia or Poland or the United States its people come from is immaterial to his sweeping argument.

In short, Huntington's monolithic approach unacceptably reduces whole complex regions to cultural or religious blocks, which renders them practically unrecognizable. Huntington's theory virtually explains nothing, and its ability to predict future conflict has been cast in serious doubt.

---

31 Galymzhan Kirbassov, 2006. "Has 'the Clash of Civilizations' Found Empirical Support?" *The Fountain* 14, no. 56 (2006). Online edition: http://www.fountainmagazine.com/article.php? ARTICLEID=783 [accessed May 24, 2010].

- 3 -
Is Islam Antipathetic to Peaceful Coexistence?

H UNTINGTON HAS POINTED TO all the wars among Muslims
and between Muslims and non-Muslims as proof that
"Islam's borders are bloody, and so are its innards."[32]
Of all the civilizations, he singled out Islam only because its
conflict with the West—as Edward Said put it—gets the lion's
share of his attention. Clashes between the West and the rest
of the world take place all the time, but it is the "fault-line
conflicts" and "core-state conflicts" with Islam that make its
relationship with the West so central.[33]

The driving force behind this conflict is obvious to
Huntington. "Wherever one looks along the perimeter of
Islam, Muslims have problems living peaceably with their
neighbors."[34] Just look at the enmity between Arabs and Jewish
people in Palestine, Indians and Pakistanis in the subcontinent,
and Muslims and Christians in Sudan, among others. These
conflicts constitute irrefutable proof of Islam's incompatibility

---

32 Huntington, *The Clash of Civilizations and the Remaking of World Order*,
258.
33 Ibid., 256
34 Ibid.

with other civilizations. Rather than try to figure out the local causes of micro events, he uses macro factors to account for them. It is much easier to argue in broad strokes that paint Islamic values as somehow intrinsically incompatible with Western articles of faith such as democracy and modernity. What is the point of bothering with *why* Muslims have not embraced, as he pretends, peaceful coexistence with Westerners?

Though elementary to historical scholarship, none of this seems to lie within Huntington's intellectual interests.

If, as he says, the clash is caused primarily by the Islamic faith's irrepressible enmity to modernity, what should we make of the West's longstanding unease with Christianity? Not only Muslims but also practicing Christians have had to live uneasily with what passes for the West's "secular ethics." Some of these ethics are radical by any historical measure. Take homosexuality, premarital sex, abortion—they are all antithetical to Christian teachings as they have been passed on for two thousand years. Huntington conveniently sidesteps this issue, because comparing Islamic and Christian ethics would undermine his whole reasoning. But this distortion cannot change the underlying reality—namely, that the clashes *within* civilizations have been far more pivotal.

This understanding is fundamental to history and the study of civilizations as viable disciplines rather than the instruments of an ideology of despair.

Huntington's opponents and proponents

Unusual for an academic, Huntington has managed to provoke worldwide controversy that has gone far beyond academic debate and permeated international relations. After former Iranian president Mohamed Khatami responded to his ideas by offering dialogue to promote peaceful coexistence among nations, the United Nations passed a resolution that declared 2001 the year of "Dialogue Among Civilizations."[35]

Let us quickly review how some scholars have argued for or against the *inevitability* of cultural collision. We are talking really about inevitability and collision here, not just "clash," which seems trivial in comparison with Huntington's grandiose claims.

Jonathan Fox set out to examine whether more clashes have occurred between Western civilizations in the post–Cold War period (when the US–Soviet rivalry created a bipolar world of power distribution) than in the pre–Cold War period (when the world became multicentered).[36] He discovered an underlying conceptual problem at the heart of the question. Views on conflicts depend very much on perspective. From an Islamic perspective, for instance, the post–Cold War period did not see more conflict. This has tended to render Huntington's theory without foundation in the eyes of Muslims. The Western perspective, on the other hand, views conflicts between Islamic and Western civilizations as growing in number, which tends to support the clash theory. Fox's findings led him to conclude that the soundness of Huntington's theory depended heavily on perspective.

Pippa Norris and Ronald Inglehart handled Huntington's thesis differently. They conducted a comparative analysis of seventy-five societies with values and beliefs that were either

---

35   United Nations Year of Dialogue Among Civilizations 2001: http://www.un.org/Dialogue/. The UN's Global Agenda for Dialogue Among Civilizations is to celebrate intellectual and cultural diversity through interaction among cultures and civilizations. The Group of Eminent Persons was appointed by the Secretary General of the United Nations with the task of working out guidelines for a dialogue among civilizations.

36   Jonathan Fox, "Two Civilizations and Ethnic Conflict: Islam and the West," *Journal of Peace Research* 38, no. 4 (2001): 459–72.

Islamic or non-Islamic.[37] Their study appeared to confirm Huntington's theory that culture *does* matter. However, they criticized the thesis for failing to identify the correct cultural fault line between Islamic and Western civilizations. They maintained that the conflict between these two civilizations has to do mainly with gender equality and sexual liberation. According to them the cultural line separating Islam from the West relates more to Eros than to Demos.[38]

Galymzhan Kirbassov has shed serious doubt on Huntington's arguments and hypotheses about the disputes that have erupted in the post–Cold War period. His findings, based on quantitative research, showed that "civilization differences do not cause interstate conflicts."[39] He used a "Probit Model" to analyze data about a total of 620 militarized interstate disputes between 1989 and 2001. Although Kirbassov found evidence of conflict between civilizations, he showed that more conflicts occurred *within* civilizations. Furthermore, whereas conflicts took place between and within some civilizations, others experienced no disputes during that period.

On Huntington, finally, Edward W. Said has observed that "history is ignored in the rush to highlight the ludicrously compressed and constricted warfare that the 'clash of civilizations' argues is the reality."[40] This is as damning a criticism as one could make of a historian.

Huntington has responded by challenging his critics to come up with a better theory to explain the disputes in the post–Cold War period. "If not civilizations, [then] what?"[41] In

37 Pippa Norris and Ronald Inglehart, "Islam & the West: Testing the 'Clash of Civilizations' Thesis" in John F. Kennedy School of Government Research Working Paper Series (No. RWP02-015), (Cambridge, MA: Harvard University, 2002).
38 Ibid., 3.
39 Kirbassov, "Has 'the Clash of Civilizations' Found Empirical Support?"
40 Edward W. Said, "The Clash of Ignorance" in *The Nation*: http://www.thenation.com/doc/20011022/said [May 24, 2010].
41 Huntington, "The Clash of Civilizations?" 186–94.

other words, if not the "clash of civilizations," then what? This is a blatant plea for us to accept his theory by default because, presumably, no other has been argued to his satisfaction.

Are there any candidates for a new theory?

One scholar, Ali Mazrui, has tried to demolish Huntington's theory and to replace it with African-American sociologist W.E.B. DuBois's view of the "clash of races" as a credible alternative to the "clash of civilizations."[42] A century ago, identifying race as major factor on the world scene, DuBois prophesied that the central issue would be "the problem of the color line."[43]

Mazrui uses three arguments that pave the way for such an interpretation.

First, if conflict among state or economic blocs is possible beyond cultural differences, then the "clash of civilizations" theory cannot be factually true. He denies that Huntington's theory contains factual truth on this point and therefore accuses the author of outright "factual fallacy."

But what makes the "clash of races" a better alternative to the "clash of civilizations"? It depends entirely on its explanatory force.

Interestingly, in his second argument Mazrui wonders if Huntington's use of the word *civilization* could not be better described as "the third stage of racial conflicts in world history." The first round of racism in world affairs led to the genocide of Native Americans and to the trans-Atlantic slave trade. He suggests that the second round might have been colonialism and imperialism. Both those stages were dominated by Western Europeans, a relatively short historical period characterized by devastating racial oppression.

Here Mazrui refers to the "conceptual fallacy" underlying

---

42   Ali A. Mazrui, *Africa and Other Civilizations: Conquest and Counter-Conquest,* ed. Ricardo Rene Laremont and Fouad Kalouche (Asmara, Eritrea: Africa World Press, 2002), 147–66.
43   Ibid., 148.

Huntington's theory, because culture and race may well share a common meaning.

In his third and last argument he argues that Huntington's theory also suffers from a "temporal fallacy." Conflicts among civilizations are not new. They have existed for centuries—during the Crusades, the trans-Atlantic slave trade, European colonization, and so on. If this is the case, then Huntington's worst mistake is "assuming that the 'clash of civilizations' lay in the future when it had, in fact, been generating tensions between Europe and the rest of the world for at least four to five hundred years."[44] The tensions—actually, bloody and deadly aggressions—were triggered by a racial paradigm: the myth of the "white race" rightfully standing on the top, the rest deservedly lying at the bottom.[45]

Which dominates the post–Cold War period, then, race or culture? If Mazrui is right that race has replaced ideology in the post–Cold War years, the ramifications lead to entirely different conclusions.[46]

Who started the clash in the first place?

Depending on the perspective, future conflicts will be triggered by cultural, religious, ideological, economic, or racial differences. W.E.B. DuBois's perspective is informed by the color line—namely, the historical forms of prejudices and discrimination experienced by the black American underclass. It represents a progressive interpretation of history that the injustice can be redressed and the course of history improved. It seeks to reveal the underlying interests at work. On the other hand, Huntington's reliance on overgeneralized, amorphous blocs of humanity may define a "culture line" of sorts, but it is a typical expression of conservatism, for which the status quo

---

44   Mazrui, *Africa and Other Civilizations*, 149–51.
45   Ibid., 151.
46   Ibid., pp. 148–49.

is the best of all worlds. It tends to camouflage the interests involved.

This said, I do not think it is meaningful to seek any simple answer to questions about which threat looms in the post–Cold War period. There are simply too many variables, and Huntington's critics have picked his theory apart precisely because of its generalities, inaccuracies, and distortions. There is no sense in producing another theory that does the same.

What bothers me most about Huntington is his refusal to recognize which actor has initiated conflict in the modern era. If conflicts are the result of a civilization clash, then it is "Western civilization" that has gone out of its way to impose slavery, colonialism, and imperialism, and to use racist ideology to justify policies of domination and displacement that are well documented in the annals of history. We are talking about one of the bloodiest and deadliest periods of history, and this is not counting the two world wars.

Which brings me to the second point. The worst "clashes" in history have occurred *within* Western civilization, too recently for Huntington to forget. There have been two catastrophic world wars, a number of murderous civil wars, and depraved totalitarian regimes (one of which lasted for three-quarters of a century). This too is part of the West's handiwork.

Third, any conflict arising from Islam's now permanent existence in the heart of the West has not been less traumatic than the experience of European Christians, religiously speaking.

These three points must be acknowledged for any rational debate to take place.

Although some empirical studies have invalidated the thesis of the "clash of civilizations," Huntington's controversial notion must not be ignored. Fact has to be distinguished from fiction. Sound analysis requires serious thought, not only about crusades and jihads but also about the mutually beneficial periods of exchange and sharing between Europe and the Islamic world on practically every level.

Muslims are heterogeneous, but paranoid demagogues like to portray them as monolithic. It may be convenient for political reasons, but compressing vast populations and regions of the world into a single, menacing entity is both morally and intellectually dishonest—more so because dialogue among civilizations cannot take place within a narrow and demeaning framework that merely perpetuates the most primitive concept of human relations: "Us against Them."

Improved dialogue among cultures, the respect of those who possess different values or simply different skin color, an end to the effort to shape the entire globe in the West's image—all these are certain to open the way for more concrete steps toward building mutual understanding.

It is not within our power to extinguish conflict altogether, but "clashes" on the scale predicted by Huntington must be avoided, not embraced and cultivated. Cooperation needs to take a new form. This is the desideratum of world peace.

PART II
Islam in the West

- 4 -

Getting Our History Straight:
Islam Is Part of Europe

WESTERN EUROPEAN COUNTRIES HAVE experienced massive influxes of migrants from Muslim countries in the last few decades. As these new arrivals have grown demographically, their faith has come under severe scrutiny. Islam has been characterized as antimodern and permanently hostile to the West and its culture. Of all other world faiths, this *religion*—as opposed to ideological, economic, or racial factors—is naturally prone to conflict with host populations. Its vitality and the overflowing zealotry of its members make it the fastest-growing religion in the West. In short, Islam is "new" to Europe, and it poses a threat to Western values and civilization.

The narrative is pretty much the same whether it is expressed in Switzerland, France, Germany, the United Kingdom, North America, or Australia. That such unfounded xenophobic claims are widespread hardly makes them true.

The reality is that Islam is *not* new in Europe. More than twenty years ago Tomas Gerholm and Yngve Lithman wrote about this topic:

Muslims have been massively present in Europe before

today. In fact, throughout the centuries Muslims have been engaged in the creation of Europe and European civilization, sometimes more actively, sometimes more passively. One could make a case of speaking of European civilizations as the Jewish-Christian-Muslim civilization. But the new factor is, firstly, that within a very short span of time Europe has received Islam as an immigrant culture carried mainly by labour migrants; secondly, that it is now being realized that the Muslims are here to stay. More than ever before Europe will be the Jewish-Christian-Muslim continent, a place where these religions and the secular ideologies derived from them come together to fight, support and fertilize each other.[47]

Unlike many intellectuals, writers, and commentators whose understanding of European history is thoroughly sanitized of Islamic contributions, Gerholm and Lithman at least make an honest effort to remind us of the Muslims' prominent role in the creation of Europe itself. Far from new to the subcontinent, Islam has been in Europe almost from the beginning.

Before examining the character of Muslim migrant influxes into the western and central parts of Europe, let us take a brief historical detour to gain a better appreciation of both the "familiarity" and "foreignness" that all three Abrahamic faiths—Christianity, Judaism, and Islam—share in Europe.

Origins of Islam

Islam was born in the Arabian Peninsula, the cradle of the ancient prophetic tradition that later gave rise to Judaism and Christianity. Muslims believe the Prophet Muhammad received his revelation through Archangel Gabriel as a *continuation of*, not in opposition to, this Abrahamic tradition. Therefore, they worship the God of Abraham no less than Christians and Jewish people do. The difference is that Muslims worship God

---

47   Tomas Gerholm and Yngve George Lithman, eds., *The New Islamic Presence in Western Europe* (London: Mansell Publishing, 1988), 3.

according to his words manifested in the Qur'an (literally "the reading"), which they consider the last revelation, and according to teachings of the last prophet (which collectively make up the Sunnah).

This granted, no other faith tradition besides Islam formally acknowledges other religions, their legitimacy, and all that they hold sacred. But that is not all. God's earlier revelations—the original Torah and Gospel—are actually reaffirmed in the Qur'an. The Qur'an says unequivocally that God gave Moses the Torah, David the *Zabur* (Psalms), Jesus the *Injil* (Gospel), and, of course, Muhammad the Qur'an (the last book revealed). The mother of Jesus, the Virgin Mary, is mentioned by name more times in the Qur'an than in the Christian Gospel. One of the six "pillars" of the Islamic creed declares belief in all the biblical prophets from Abraham down to Moses and Jesus; another calls for acceptance of God's revelations to them.

Besides the six pillars of faith, there are the five pillars of Islam, relating mostly to matters of ritual: *shahada* (bearing witness to the oneness of God and the prophethood of Muhammad); *salat* (praying five times a day facing Mecca); *sawm Ramadan* (fasting from sunrise and sunset for the month of Ramadan); *zakat* (almsgiving to the poor if one has the means); and hajj (making the pilgrimage to Mecca at least once in a lifetime, if possible). There are many similar rituals and beliefs in both Judaism and Christianity.

No wonder then that Prophet Muhammad should insist that his purpose was not to introduce a new religion. Western scholars who know something about or are experts in Islam fully recognize this. Immanuel Willerstein took note of the early Muslims' claim "that they had built on the wisdom they had inherited from Jews and Christians with a new and truly final form of commitment to Allah."[48] This is not to say that there are no differences among the People of the Book (Muslims,

48 Immanuel Willerstein, "Islam, the West, and the World," *Journal of Islamic Studies* (Oxford: Oxford University Press, 1999), 111.

Jewish people, and Christians). The bulk of the differences between Muslims and Christians revolve around doctrinal matters relating to the Trinity and Crucifixion, not to mention those of a ritualistic nature such as prayer, diet, and so on.

Beyond these there is a lot of continuity with Christian tradition, extending even to the cultural sphere. For example, the early Christian churches had developed a system of bishoprics with administrative and civil functions. Muslims developed similar patterns of administration, which quickly evolved into a full-fledged social, economic, political, and military order reaching far beyond their geographic origins. The patterns sometimes resembled the *servi Caesari* of the Roman Empire and the *ministeriales* (in medieval Germany) in Europe.

Moreover, Muslims fought and governed, traded, and intermarried with people of other faiths, built and settled until the entire civilized world became joined under the aegis of Islamic civilization. In Christian-majority regions such as the old Syria and Egypt, Christians for centuries helped run the local bureaucracies.

Although the early years of Islam saw mainly Arab Muslims, the demography rapidly changed as the Umayyad caliphate continued to expand across Asia, North Africa, and the Iberian Peninsula. The army of Caliph Yazid Al-Wahid was first to set foot on European soil, in 711, barely a century after Islam was introduced, in a southern Spanish town called Xeres.[49] This contact brought unprecedented social and economic transformation in the Iberian Peninsula, marginalized and suppressed as it had been by Imperial Rome in earlier times.

Literature, arts, science, and theology blossomed in the heartland of Islam as cosmopolitan society took shape on a scale the world had never seen before. It may even be said that the first foundations of "globalism" were laid thanks to the tempo and depth of exchanges between Muslims and

---

49 Robert J. Pauly, *Islam in Europe: Integration or Marginalization?* (Hants, England: Ashgate, 2004), 127.

corners of the world hitherto thought too far-flung from the Mediterranean hub. Muslim tradesmen traveled the world, and because they did, they amassed a unique practical knowledge of geography that proved absolutely critical to the later rise of the European powers. With respect to learning, the earliest university-type institution, called *Bayt al-Hikma* (House of Wisdom), was established in Baghdad as early as the ninth century. It sponsored the study of rhetoric, logic, metaphysics, theology, algebra, geometry, trigonometry, physics, biology, medicine, and surgery.[50]

Inevitably, a massive transfer of knowledge began to take place from every scientific and intellectual field early on to the Christian-ruled parts of Europe. Muslim learning was highly coveted and Islamic civilization a model to be emulated in every respect—except religion, of course.

The number of Muslims today stands at more than 1.5 billion worldwide. In Europe alone there are 49 million out of a population of 735 million. The numbers are still growing,[51] even though "European Muslims represent a mere three percent of the population of the continent, hardly the numbers to ensure a Muslim take-over of Europe."[52]

That is 3 percent! It is still significant, if only because it dates back so many centuries. But the presence of Muslims today is dismissed as a fluke of history that must be feared and controlled. Islam has been in Europe since at least the eighth century, but it is still somehow foreign.

---

50   S. E. Al-Djazairi, *The Golden Age and Decline of Islamic Civilization* (Manchester, England: Bayt al Hikma Press, 2006), 160.
51   Houssein Kettani: 2010:24. According to the 2008 World Economic Forum annual report, the "percentage of Muslim population in the EU-15 is expected to rise from 4.3% in 2006 to approximately 10% to 15% by 2025, with a higher concentration in urban areas of up to 30% in countries such as France, Germany and Holland," 5.
52   Shada Islam, "Beyond Minarets: Europe's Growing Problem with Islam: Can One Be Both European and Muslim?" in *YaleGlobal* Online: http://yaleglobal.yale.edu/content/beyond-minarets-europes-growing-problem [accessed September 24, 2010].

But why is Islam foreign and not Christianity or Judaism? They too originated in the southwest of the Asian continent. Christianity is said to be "universal" and Islam "Eastern." True, Christianity has expanded to the far reaches of the earth through empire and organized mission in the main,[53] but to the average Westerner this still qualifies Christendom as a universal religion. Islam is different; it properly belongs to the Arabs of the Middle East. It is a gross distortion of reality, one that has its roots in the long-standing relationship of conflict between two "civilizations." The balance is such that any encroachment by Islam constitutes an "invasion."

This relationship predates the Cold War, as Huntington says; therefore, it did not just pop into being out of nowhere. Looking at it through the lens of different periods of history, the conflict that lies at the heart of it has a distinct modern flavor, and for good reason. The modern period clearly shows that "the chief cultural transgressor has throughout been the Western world"; it included conquest, occupation, slavery, and colonization.[54] Western Europe had simply decided it needed to dominate Islamic lands, but in so doing, it brought those lands even closer to them than before.

Thanks to this relatively recent relationship of domination, and because the European powers had attempted to carve out a sphere of influence and dependencies for themselves, Muslims began to migrate to Europe after the colonial era drew to a close.

---

53   The British Empire alone dominated about a quarter of the world's land. The figure of Jesus Christ was used in their mission, with the Queen more a symbol. A South African song laments how the British arrived with the Bible in the lands of the natives and exchanged the Bible for the land they took from the natives.

54   Ali A. Mazrui, "Western Values and The Satanic Verses," in *Debating the African Condition: Ali Mazrui and His Critics*, eds. Alamin M. Mazrui and Willy M. Mutunga (Asmara, Eritrea: Africa World Press, 2004), vol. 1, 11–12.

European identity from the beginning

It is easy to forget that Muslim-Christian relations were not always like this.

Historically, the "European" identity began to take shape in earnest a century after the birth of the Prophet of Islam. It too developed in the shadow of conflict with Muslims, but there is much more to this chapter than war and enmity. The first significant opportunity for Islam-Christendom exchange outside the Islamic world, which already teemed with Christians, took place while Muslims governed the multiethnic, multiconfessional Iberian Peninsula. A European identity was intended to counter their predominance there and to forge an exclusively "Christian" European zone.[55]

But this was only the negative, military path by which Muslims left their imprint on European identity. Islam actually began to shape the future of "Europe" as soon as the Prophet Muhammad and his first followers joined the Abrahamic family and thereby brought together deep historical trends already at work that traced far back into the distant past.

The world is far more interconnected than we commonly believe. The European identity has many roots. Here is a bird's-eye view of the global transformations that have fed the identity that many in the West today take for granted.

---

55 Robert J. Pauly, *Islam in Europe: Integration or Marginalization?* (Hants, England: Ashgate, 2004), 129.

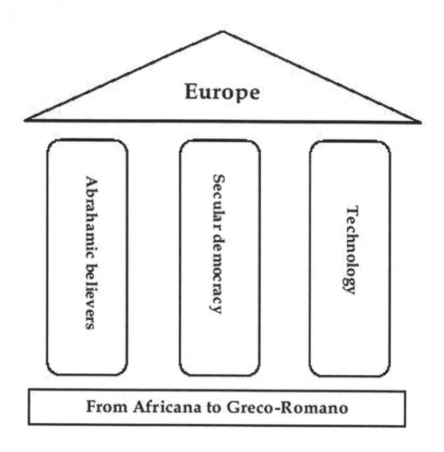

Diagram 1: The Makers of Europe

Most paleoanthropologists consider Africa the oldest inhabited territory on Earth, the original home of *Homo sapiens*. In antiquity, the Greco-Romanized northern coast of the Mediterranean maintained links with it that have not since been interrupted. Though relatively more isolated than the Arabian Peninsula, Africa too was brought into the fold.

Given all these roots, how could anyone think of the West as being simply Judeo-Christian, and that Islam is foreign? Islam is a pure expression of the Abrahamic tradition and the premodern world that was born in the seventh century. Historically, this allowed it to play a pivotal role in resuscitating

Christianity itself, when the latter was actually losing ground, not gaining. Given this deep affinity and "kinship," the old denials about the place of Islam within the Abrahamic tradition cannot stand. Indeed, "just as it is widely acknowledged that the current meaning of a Judeo-Christian tradition was forged during World War II, today there is growing recognition of the existence of a Judeo-Christian-Islamic tradition, embracing all the children of Abraham."[56]

But exclusion is an old game that has refused to go away even as the West flaunts its modern ways and modern society. Today, hot wars erupt as high technology transforms our world into a global village; democracies diversify at the same time that ultranationalists sink to new levels of intellectual depravity and Islamophobia. *East versus West! Islam is the religion of foreigners! It doesn't belong here.*

It is always a risky game deciding how far one should go to reclaim the past in the name of identity. By the time the Europeans discovered the rough features of the identity by which we know them today, Muslims had already been governing the Iberian Peninsula for seven and a half centuries. This, *after* they were stopped in 732 by the army of Charles Martel in the French province of Aquitaine, and again by his son Pépin, twenty-seven years later at Narbonne. Although these two military defeats failed to reverse the march of history, they still "provided the foundation for the construction of a Christian-oriented Western European sub-continental empire under the tutelage of the standard bearer of the family's third generation—the Carolingian Emperor Charlemagne."[57] To fight the Islamic threat, Charlemagne sought to unite Western Europe and gave it a common "Christian" identity. Christians fought holy wars against Muslims, and Muslims fought jihad against Christians.

---

56 John L. Esposito and Dalia Mogahed, *Who Speaks for Islam? What a Billion Muslims Really Think* (New York: Gallup Press, 2007), 8.
57 Pauly, *Islam in Europe*, 126.

The illusions and exclusions of identity

Although they provided ample opportunity also for positive exchanges,[58] medieval Muslim-Christian confrontations led to fanatical, bloody efforts to impose uniform order upon Europe. This effort lasted for several centuries and began with the Muslims, who were finally expelled from Spain, forcibly converted or killed. Then two dominant rulers rose on the subcontinent, Napoleon Bonaparte and Adolf Hitler, who tried to complete the "cleansing" through military domination.[59]

In our times the European Union marks a new, relatively benign stage in the historic effort to unite Europe. But does European unification necessarily have to imply uniformity? Is it realistic to think in these terms—or desirable, for that matter?

Articles 21 and 22 of the Swiss Federal Constitution on equality ban discrimination based on "sex, race, ethnic or social origin, genetic features, language, religion, belief, political or any opinion, membership of a national minority, property, birth, disability, age or sexual orientation." If this position is as inclusive as it sounds, then everyone—from government cabinet ministers to religious leaders, from transnational organizations to local communities—should be able to regard Muslims as part of Europe, not as a foreign element no one is quite sure what to do about.

On the other hand, the Muslims of Western Europe need to put their community in order. As difficult as it is, perhaps the most important task is to reshape Islam within a unique historical moment. Muslims cannot afford to perpetuate their current situation or accept it *amor fati*. They have to rise above their own version of cultural exclusionism, embrace the universal principles of Islam, and then turn reinvigorated to

---

58   In Córdoba for example, Christian subjects were "tolerated, protected and treated with charity" by the caliphate (Smith, 1999: 329). They also traded, and exchanged knowledge.
59   Pauly, *Islam in Europe*, 136.

the task of tackling the demands of the world in which they live.

This will not destroy their faith. On the contrary, it will strengthen it to a point where they can feel at home both as Muslims and citizens. True, by immigrating to Western countries they effectively renounced the collective comfort of living in Muslim-majority countries. Becoming a minority has provoked a serious identity crisis among many youth and their parents alike by virtue of this new environment. But identity crisis is typical of almost every type of immigrant community, not just Muslim. And identity searching is normal to every youth. Before becoming a minority, Muslims had no need to question themselves deeply on who they are and why they are here. This was mostly taken for granted. In most Muslim countries it is normal for women to cover themselves from head to toe. Mosques are found everywhere; there are many tall minarets, and *adhān* is called five times a day. During Ramadan restaurants are expected to close in the daytime, sometimes for the whole month.

On the other side, Europeans find tattooed skin on a man and a pierced navel on a skimpily dressed woman perfectly normal. To them it is long-bearded, praying men and fully covered woman that are out of the ordinary. Each side reacts to the other, but the main victims are still Muslims when public figures treat migrants and immigrants as *Fremden* (aliens). They are diasporas and will remain so by virtue of nothing more than their ethnicity and religion.

The natural reflex of Muslims is to congregate with others of their faith, no matter where they come from. Muslims love their *ummah* (community in Islam) and seek comfort in knowing they have one. But then everybody seeks comfort in a larger collectivity of shared beliefs, values, language, ethnicity, and so on, including non-Muslim immigrants. It is simply human nature. Human beings need to belong.

In Europe, their identity has crystallized into a new

community of shared religious values, but one that unfortunately is neither here nor there. Although Muslims recognize the centrality of European citizenship in their lives, merging Islamic with Western values continues to be a major challenge. Citizenship touches on an aspect of collective identity over which every nation has had to struggle in the modern age. In this respect the presence of Muslims is only the latest element in the political and cultural dynamics of modern-day Europe.

In fact, if the status, meaning, and implications of citizenship are still unclear to European Muslims, they have been a challenge even in their countries of origin. Consider this. In the same year, 2010, that France's lower house of parliament banned the veil that covers the woman's face in public, Syria's minister of higher education issued a policy outlawing the face cover in all the universities. The niqāb (which leaves only the eyes uncovered) and the burka (which also conceals the eyes with a mesh panel) have been banished from many Arab countries. Turkey banned the hijāb (headscarf) from its universities and public buildings back in the 1980s. France, a militantly secularist state, imposed a blanket public ban on all religious symbols, Muslims or other, from public schools in 2004, and in 2011 wearing the burka in public was banned.

The Muslims of Europe have no alternative but to chart their own path, within the value boundaries negotiated between Islam and the secular state—which, in principle, is pledged to the rights protection for all citizens without exception.

- 5 -
Four Pivotal Events

MUSLIM COMMUNITIES IN EUROPE today face a number of challenges because of societal exclusion, economic distress, and crime. When they become acute, the resulting social ills have the potential to trigger social unrest. France, in particular, has experienced periodic riots in the *banlieues*, or suburbs, of cities such as Lyon and Marseille. The most easily identifiable culprit has been well known: unemployment.

The conventional wisdom is that a serious tackling of stubborn unemployment would lead to more social tranquility. But the creation of employment alone is not enough to dampen widespread discontent among French Muslim youth. Other issues gain importance when the cultural and religious needs of Muslims are systematically ignored at the local, regional, and national levels. Muslims desire halāl butcheries and separate Muslim schools, but their detractors have interpreted these as an attempt to build a parallel society.

Why has the fear of Muslim aspirations become so generalized? Are native French or Swiss to blame, or the Muslims?

Before getting to that part of the problem, which lies within

Muslim communities themselves, let me point to an unsettling confluence of external forces that lies beyond the control of both the Muslims and their European hosts. It has compounded the situation, because no matter how apolitical Muslims try to make their religion, the issue of "Islam"—to put it bluntly— has turned into a political football. This situation has kept Muslims and non-Muslims alike from getting a handle on their relationship and dealing seriously with practical issues. Instead, demagoguery is given free rein and periodically leads to authoritarian decisions from on high.

I have identified four events that have set the stage for the unprecedented level of demagoguery we have witnessed in recent years on *both* sides. They have had the net effect of burying the more positive aspects of Europe's long-standing historic relationship with Islam.

1. The September 11, 2001, terrorist attacks on the United States.

2. Publication of Salman Rushdie's *The Satanic Verses*.

3. The Dutch film *Submission*.

4. The Danish caricature of the Prophet Mohammad.

Not only were the thrust and character of these events deeply offensive to Muslims, but they caused social strife in several countries. Lives were lost. Each event produced two distinct groups: one that felt deeply offended, another that was shocked.

The worst event to take place saw a group of terrorists hijacking four airplanes in the name of Islam (fifteen from Saudi Arabia, two from the United Arab Emirates, and an Egyptian). They targeted the World Trade Center in New York (a symbol of American economic prowess) and the Pentagon in Washington, D.C. (a symbol of American military prowess).

A fourth plane was brought down in Pennsylvania that may have been headed for the White House (a symbol of American political prowess). They managed to inflict a deep wound in the American psyche, leaving other nations equally in horror. It is easy to forget that Christians were *not* the primary target of the attack. No church or cathedral was damaged. Instead, three thousand people of every nationality and religion died. The primary motivation of the terrorists was to strike at the "US Empire."

Whatever their grievances against the United States and its policies, this act was roundly condemned by Muslims around the globe. Those Muslims who celebrated it, with bin Laden, justified the mass murder by pointing to the Western "Christian" armies stationed in Saudi Arabia and to the plight of the Palestinian people. Bin Laden linked the attack to the dispossession of the Palestinians and the threat to Mecca.[60]

Interestingly, when asked about what pains them and what they seek to remedy in their world, the vast majority of Muslims point to precisely these two general and pivotal issues. But does this make them terrorists or even potential terrorists?

The other event that heightened tensions between Muslims and non-Muslims across the world was the publication of Salman Rushdie's novel. Muslims universally—both fundamentalist and secular—agreed that *The Satanic Verses* defamed Islam, and in one voice they declared it blasphemous.[61] The very title of the book, which referred to the content of the Qur'an as "Satanic Verses" and thus the work of the Devil, demonstrated abuse. If it is true that the Bible is the most widely read book in translation, then the Qur'an is the most widely recited book (five times a day) in the language in which it was originally

---

60   Nasr Hamid Abu Zaid, "Der Islam in Europa: Eine Krise des Wissens oder des Dialogs,?" in *Die Arabische Welt: Zwischen Tradition und Moderne,* ed. Khalid Al-Maaly (Heidelberg: Palmyra Verlag, 2004), 35.
61   Mazrui, "Western Values and The Satanic Verses," 148.

revealed and written down. Islamic devotion is not about banning or prosecuting writers simply because they want to express their opinions. But nor is it about people enriching themselves at the expense of the dignity of others.

Rushdie clearly wanted to create doubt about the authenticity of the Qur'an and to create publicity for himself.[62] He went so far as to portray the wives of the Prophet of Islam as prostitutes.[63] This was tantamount to telling Christians that the Virgin Mary was a prostitute and that Jesus was the bastard son of a prostitute. The latter, incidentally, would have been just as insulting to Muslims, as Jesus is a central prophet in the Qur'an. Hardly surprising, then, that Rushdie's work should be taken as a provocation masquerading as freedom of expression.[64]

The third controversy grew out of the short 2004 film *Submission*, broadcast by a Dutch public network. Somali refugee and Dutch MP Ayaan Hirsi Ali produced it with filmmaker Theo van Gogh.[65] They portrayed four Muslim women whose almost naked bodies exhibited verses from the Qur'an. The film, which Ruud Peters and Sipco Vellenga agreed

---

62   Salman Rushdie, *The Satanic Verses* (New York: Viking Press, 1989), 363–68.

63   Ibid., 380–83.

64   Book burnings took place throughout the Muslim world. On British soil, where Salman Rushdie is a citizen, there were demonstrations by burning a copy of the book in the city of Bradford (Pauly, 2004:95). In India, his country of origin, *The Satanic Verses* is banned with the support of distinguished Hindu, Sikh, Christian, and Muslim intellectuals (Mazrui, 2004:162). South Africa, Pakistan, and a number of Middle Eastern countries also banned the book. Pakistanis protested, "It is as if Rushdie had composed a brilliant poem about the private parts of his parents, and then recited the poem in the market place to the cheers and laughter of strangers! These strangers then paid him money for all the jokes about his parents' genitalia" (Mazrui, 2004:145).

65   Ayaan Hirsi Ali believes that "true" Muslims are a threat to the free Western world, and Theo van Gogh routinely called Muslims "goatfuckers" (see Wohlrab-Sahr/Tezcan, *Konfliktfeld Islam in Europa*, 2007, 221).

was "deliberately meant to provoke Muslims,"[66] resulted in the brutal death of Theo van Gogh in Amsterdam at the hands of a Moroccan-Dutch man named Mohammed Bouyeri. The killer shot and stabbed him before cutting his throat ritually. Two knives pinning a message to the victim's chest threatened Hirsi Ali with death.

As offended as Muslim believers were by the film, this murder so shocked the entire Dutch society that the resulting tensions led to attacks on mosques and Islamic schools.[67]

The last controversy had an effect similar to the Rushdie affair. On September 30, 2005, the Danish *Jyllandsposten* published twelve cartoons that, among other things, showed the Prophet Muhammad with a bomb in his turban. The image dismayed the Muslim community. Like Rushdie, the journalist in question exhibited astonishing insensitivity, but the failure of judgment extended to those who sanctioned the cartoons' publication. The net effect was, again, violence and several deaths around the world.

Was this Danish journalist using or abusing his "freedom of expression"? What was the purpose of creating offensive cartoons that linked common stereotypes of Muslims to what was purest and cherished above all else in their religion? By depicting the Prophet as a terrorist the journalist wanted to test how far he could go. But why? Was the newspaper's circulation plummeting? Even so, are economic considerations sufficient reason for insult and injury?

If freedom of expression were alone in question, why are Christians and Jewish people not also tarred in public? We know that the same *Jyllandsposten* that trumpets "freedom of expression" rejected "a series of unsolicited cartoons offering a lighthearted take on the resurrection of Christ" from a Danish

---

66   Monika Wohlrab-Sahr and Levent Tezcan (Hrsg.), *Konfliktfeld Islam in Europa*, Soziale Welt, Sonderband 17 (Baden-Baden, Germany: Nomos, 2007), 221.
67   Wohlrab-Sahr/Tezcan, *Konfliktfeld Islam in Europa*, 221.

illustrator, claiming they might provoke an outcry.[68] What I gather from this is that although freedom of expression has to give ground when the depiction debases Jesus, it is essential in the case of Muhammad, the prophet of a "foreign religion." A cartoon as offensive as that of Prophet Muhammad, depicting Queen Elizabeth, for example, has yet to appear in her kingdom's "free press."

Even more surprising was the Danish prime minister's refusal to enter into dialogue with his Muslim compatriots on this or any other issue. After boycotts, violence, and complaints to the UN, a "dialogue" of sorts finally took place. It ended with the standard "apology": "We deeply regret that you found this offensive."[69]

Unsustainable misconceptions

Because a handful of Muslims acted and spoke in the name of Islam in the course of these four events, Islam became almost inextricably associated with horrific violence in the public eye. More terrorist attacks followed 9/11—e.g., Spain in March 2004, London in July 2005—further eroding Islam's image and generating hatred for the Muslims residing in the West. Regardless of where one lays the blame for the violence, the public has come to see Islam as a violent religion.

This sentiment found extreme expression among people bent on attacking Muslims and their religion. Geert Wilders, a Dutch parliamentarian and prominent critic of Islam, promptly produced a short clip called *Fitna*, his aim being to illustrate how Islam itself encouraged violence. In 2009, a group of Christian fundamentalists in Florida were so fired up with zealotry that they planned an "International Burn-a-Qur'an Day" to commemorate the ninth anniversary of 9/11. Before being persuaded by public officials and the public outcry that

---

68   Johan Galtung, *50 Years: 100 Peace & Conflict Perspectives* (Bergen: Kolofon forlag, 2008), 234.
69   Ibid., 234–35.

followed, they did their best to denigrate Islam as a "religion of the Devil." To them the Qur'an is a satanic book that incites violence against Christians. In 2011 pastor Terry Jones and his followers at last burned a copy of the Qur'an. However, this brought no reaction from anywhere apart from Afghanistan. Not only Terry Jones but many others must be perplexed by the development. Muslims are on the streets with *go out* slogan not for Obama but meant for Ben Ali Saleh, Mubarak, Gaddafi, Saleh, Assad, and the rest to step down from leadership. They seek the pursuit of freedom, not burning the American flag or the Bible. The Al Jazeera news channel calls it *the Arab Awakening*.

In view of these and numerous similar reactions why not simply accept the existence of a civilizational clash? And why not consider the desire of Muslims for special schools and mosques the cutting edge of a Muslim onslaught?

This kind of approach is double edged. What prevents Muslims, in turn, from regarding the United Nations as an international venue for the worldwide Western onslaught on them? After all, four of the five permanent members sitting on the UN Security Council are not only nominally "Christian" but European states (the United States, France, Britain, and Russia). Such a conclusion may be termed as simplistic, but Mazrui has characterized the UN as a White Man's Club with nonwhite visitors.[70]

The truth is that, in the twenty-first century, Muslims cannot be dismissed so cavalierly. This is not to say that there aren't strong currents of Muslim "fundamentalism" aspiring to a return to a set of (reformulated) core beliefs and a lost age they idealize as the "purest." There are also Muslim terrorists who use violence as a means to "purify" the *ummah* (community in Islam) and to prepare for such a return. But fundamentalists and terrorists, both purely modern phenomena, hardly prove

---

70 Mazrui, *Islam: Between Globalization and Counterterrorism* (Asmara, Eritrea: Africa World Press, 2006), 280.

the widespread misperception that Islam is completely in consonance with their nefarious aims.

Muslims come from diverse traditions and have made crucial historical contributions to humanity. Moreover, they have demonstrated a marked interest in dialogue across cultures and borders. The United Nations declared 2001 the "Year of Dialogue Among Civilizations" thanks to the efforts of Mohammad Khatami, then president of Iran, who introduced the idea in response to Huntington's thesis.

If French, German, and British citizens without exception are to enjoy stability, Robert J. Pauly recommends, achieving a more equitable and socially and politically stable society requires four steps.[71] The first is to acknowledge the significance of the problem. Second is to facilitate, rather than stifle, the interaction between younger Muslims and their cohorts in the suburbs with a view toward eliminating negative stereotypes. Third, the interaction among various ethnic and religious groups has to deepen the integration process at the micro-level. Finally, we must use positive local outcomes as a model for regional and national progress.

This view sounds promising. What we need is the will to take us there.

---

71   Pauly, *Islam in Europe*, 59–60, 88–90, and 118–122.

PART III
Muslims of Western Europe

- 6 -
France, Germany, and
the United Kingdom

F RANCE
With roughly 3.5 to 5 million Muslims, France is home
to the largest Muslim population in Western Europe.[72]
That is 6 to 8.5 percent of a total population of 58.5 million, the
largest minority in the country. They are mainly of Moroccan,
Tunisian, and Algerian descent. It is no coincidence that France
had tried hard to colonize large parts of North Africa and to
dominate the rest through other means. After World War II,
it experienced great demand for labor. This, combined with
decolonization (1956–62) and the outbreak of the Algerian
Civil War (1962–65), triggered large migratory waves.[73] All
that migrant workers needed to bring with them was some
knowledge of French; their labor was needed the most.

The result of this cheap labor from the Maghreb drove the
French industrial engine. Segregated from French society in
government-subsidized hostels, however, these guest workers

72 These figures are from Euro-Islam.info (http://www.euro-islam.
info), a network of researchers and scholars who conduct comparative
research on Islam and Muslims in the West. This organization
disseminates information to politicians, the media, and the public.
73 Pauly, *Islam in Europe*, 36.

accustomed themselves to a short stay while dreaming of a more prosperous future when they returned to their home countries. The less realistic this return seemed, the more they sought to reunify their families. The first generation raised the next, until they all began to see themselves as both Muslim and French.

Although many migrants held French passports, especially the young, they faced poor economic conditions. Compared with other minority groups Muslims experienced more discrimination. They were prevented from running their own schools. Although France had a public policy of supporting schools run by religious communities, Muslim requests were routinely turned down. And the Muslim community found little support to build mosques in which to worship like any normal religious community. The result is that France has very few official, cathedral-like mosques. Instead, worshippers have to pray in garages and apartments turned into prayer rooms.

Germany

As in France, Muslims make up Germany's largest and fastest-growing religious minority. Euro-Islam.info, a network of researchers on Islam and Muslims in the West, has estimated that there are about 3 to 3.5 million Muslims, 70 percent of whom are of Turkish origin, as part of the government policy of planned migration to augment the domestic labor force. Thanks to a chronic lack of labor to drive economic growth, a pact was signed for Turkey (1961), Tunisia and Morocco (1965), and the former Yugoslavia (1968) to facilitate the entry of laborers. As in France, the initial groups of workers were soon joined by spouses, children, and other family members, transforming temporary workers into permanent residents. Muslims today come from a wide range of ethnic backgrounds and have migrated to Germany for various purposes.[74] There are, in addition, around 100,000 native German converts to Islam. But

74   Pauly, *Islam in Europe*, 65–93.

the change of status from guest workers to permanent residents was especially ill received. Many native Germans regarded mosque building and Muslim associations as an attempt to insert an alien cultural identity. Germans had long valued their relative homogeneity and now saw their "Germanness" as threatened.

The consequences of all these forces soon became clear. Muslims were so socially marginalized that even some third-generation Turks had insufficient knowledge of German, though they were born and raised in Germany. They repeated the pattern begun by their parents who, living in barracks and confined to unskilled jobs, had little opportunity to interact with ordinary Germans.

United Kingdom

In Britain there are roughly 1.6 million Muslims, who make up 2.7 percent of the total population, the largest and fastest-growing religious minority. Although diverse, the vast majority of them are Pakistani, Bangladeshi, and Indian.

Muslims here have had a long history. They first came three hundred years ago as sailors known as *lascars*. In Cardiff, Yemenis built one of the first mosques in 1870. Just like the North Africans in France and the Turks in Germany, today's British Muslims helped fuel local industries at a critical time in the global economy. The only difference is that they were not government sponsored, but recruited privately.[75] Other than that, they lived inside similar types of homogeneous housing enclaves, and had little contact with ordinary British people. Most of them planned to return home someday, but they ended up gathering their family from abroad, marrying, and having children. The difference is that they were better able to develop community infrastructures that served their specific needs as a religious community, establishing mosques and halāl meat

---

75   Pauly, *Islam in Europe*, 95–126.

outlets. As they did, minority-majority cleavages appeared and grew wider.

Although the unemployment rate is more prevalent among them than in the larger population, Muslims—especially from the Asian subcontinent—appear to be relatively more successful than their counterparts in France and Germany. They hold management positions, enjoy professional careers (as accountants, solicitors, doctors, engineers), and own businesses (shops, restaurants, hotels, real estate). There are also Muslim parliamentarians and Lord Mayors. There is even an Islamic Party of Britain.

Although most British Muslims have adopted a modernistic outlook, some reject Western secular values altogether, preferring to live within a strict interpretation of the Qur'an (e.g., *Hizb-ut-Tahrir*/Organization for seeking a unify Islamic rule and *Tablighi Jama'at*/Society for spreading Islamic faith). With the decolonization of the British Empire came the first waves of migration, which fueled the postwar British economy by filling the demand for cheap, blue-collar labor. Later, however, people seeking refuge from government persecution of minority groups in Kenya, Somalis escaping war-ravaged zones, and Pakistanis and Indians fleeing skirmishes in Kashmir constituted a sizable proportion of the new arrivals.

- 7 -
Switzerland

THE DYNAMICS LET LOOSE by the Muslim presence in Western
Europe have developed according to a pattern similar
throughout the region. As one group vilified *all* Muslims,
not just some, its counter-group rose in aggressive response,
followed by a third group—larger than the first—who were
shocked by the response.

Background to Switzerland's present crisis

This said, each country offers unique conditions and
challenges. Switzerland happens also to be one of the richest
countries in the world, some of its cities ranking highest for
quality of life. Moreover, it is celebrated for its long tradition
of "direct democracy."

The Federal Constitution of 1848 uses the Latin name
Confoederatio Helvetica (Helvetic Confederation), which is also
engraved on the pediment of the Federal Palace in Bern. The
Confoederatio Helvetica refers to a federal republic that aspires
to full citizenship for its people, no exceptions. A major
instrument of Swiss direct democracy is based on *droits civiques*
(or civil rights) defined and granted in 1848 with respect to the
submission of constitutional initiatives and referenda. These
rights provided the basis upon which it was decided that the

Swiss Constitution had to be amended specifically to allow for a ban on the construction of minarets. It happened in orderly fashion through the November 2009 referendum, christened *"Gegen den Bau von Miratten"* ("Against the Construction of Minarets"). Although the Swiss Federal Council (*der Bundesrat*) and the parliament later recommended that the proposed amendment be rejected, the measure was approved by 57.5 percent of voters.

The main politicians responsible for this victory came from the *Schweizerischen Volkspartei* (Swiss People's Party [SVP]) and the *Eidgenössischen Demokratischen Union* (Federal Democratic Union [EDU]). Their views became fully constitutional—and *law*.

These developments did not occur out of the blue. The groundwork had been prepared for some time. As Islamophobia began to permeate Swiss politics, conservative magazine *Die Weltwoche* decided to publish the Danish cartoons in question. This was not a simple case of xenophobia, but more specifically one of *Islamophobia*, now an immovable feature of right-wing politicians across the country. Then in 2004, placards warning of the Islamic *Überfremdung* (foreign infiltration), or invasion, helped launch an initiative against the automatic naturalization of foreigners and the alleged naturalization of Muslim terrorists.

The proponents of this last initiative propagated a particularly repulsive image: a Swiss identity card (ID) together with Bin Laden. Five years later the campaign seeking a ban on the construction of minarets pictured minarets as missiles. The committee heading the campaign claimed to oppose the construction of minarets because they saw it as a power symbol of Islam (*Machtsymbol*) and of ongoing Islamization. On Swiss soil, it represented "creeping Islamization" (*schleichende Islamisierung*).

Opponents of the initiative insisted that the ban would prove an impediment to dialogue, because they saw mosque construction with minarets as part of religious freedom. More fundamentally, mosques and minarets had to do with identity, no worse or better than religious construction in any other religious community.

As the debate grew nationwide, Muslims continued to maintain a peaceful posture, despite the heated exchanges. A secondary controversy was on freedom of expression and censorship. SVP/EDU's inflammatory posters depicting minarets as missiles were prohibited in cities and cantons after the Federal Commission against Racism judged them a denigration and defamation of peaceful Swiss people (*Verunglimpfung und Diffarmierung der friedlichen Schweizer Beölkerung*).

Both the debates and referendum vote provoked a variety of reactions abroad, and Swiss banks feared retaliatory measures emanating from the Arab world. The opponents of the minaret ban raised concerns about religious peace in Switzerland. Some even demanded that the final vote be declared null and void, believing the initiative contradicted the basic principles of the Swiss Federal Constitution and the European Convention on Human Rights (ECHR). However, the proponents saw no violation of either religious freedom or international law. Subsequently, the SVP bluntly demanded that the referendum be fully implemented and threatened to introduce a new referendum if the results were annulled.

The ban initiative illustrates how contentious the relationship between the Muslim communities and at least part of the host society has become. The inflammatory placards alone were telling. Depicting a woman in a burka with minarets like missiles reflected the prevailing level of ignorance about Islam in Swiss society at the time. Clearly, the fear of Islam was too generalized for rational debate. That Islam was monolithic and totally at odds with Western values and norms suddenly became law.

Despite their disillusionment, most Muslims accepted the

results and the fact that it pretty well painted them with the same brushstroke. While right-wingers celebrated their victory, Switzerland's Muslims called for demonstrations to voice their utter disapproval of violence, and against Gaddafi who called for a jihad against their country.

The particularities of Swiss Muslims

Swiss Muslims have to be lauded for steadfastly shunning all forms of violence in the face of the hostility all around them. Perhaps they truly believe in Johan Galtung's most essential basis for conflict transformation that peace should be achieved by peaceful means. But then, *Islam* itself means "peace." If there is one respect in which Muslims are monolithic, it is that they believe in and aspire to peaceful coexistence.

Genesis and growth of the Muslim communities

There are presently about 400,000 Muslims in Switzerland, roughly 90 percent of whom are of Yugoslav or Turkish origin. Their numbers, representing around 5 percent of the population, are more than enough to justify government attention at the cantonal, not just the national, level to help ensure peaceful coexistence in an increasingly ethnically and religiously diverse society.

Initially, the two main large-scale waves of Muslim migrants to Switzerland occurred in the early sixties and the second half of the seventies. The first, mainly from Turkey and former Yugoslavia, was triggered by a strong demand for *Gastarbeiter* (guest workers), not unlike other Western European states. Besides guest workers there also came political exiles from the Middle East and both North and sub-Saharan Africa. Alongside them, workers from Italy, Spain, and Portugal also streamed into the country.

Switzerland—which lacked the labor force to advance its economy—reckoned these workers to be hardworking and welcomed them all. Everyone profited: cheap foreign laborers drove the economy forward and, in return, enjoyed new opportunities to help their families back home. But the goal, all along, was to fill a *temporary* shortfall in domestic manpower and then these recruits, predominately young *ledigen* (celibate) men, would return to their countries. As it turned out, most of them stayed on, the first wave triggering a second one, this time made up of family members. As in the case of the North Africans in France, the Pakistanis and Bangladeshis in Britain, and the Turks in Germany, Switzerland's Balkan and Turkish laborers took advantage of the legal right to seek reunification with their families and the single men among them to bring their new brides over to Switzerland. By the second half of the seventies the new migrant population basically included two generations.

Family reunification led to two important developments:

First, because migrant workers continued to live inside special compounds even with their families, contact with the larger Swiss society became less urgent. Social isolation, however, is never ideal in the best of circumstances. It induced some to think about returning home, but the weight of family responsibilities quickly turned this into a pipe dream. They had already become a reality in Swiss society. Nevertheless, remaining isolated was equally unrealistic. They needed services such as maternity care, schooling, and mosques; garages and halls used as tiny prayer spaces were hardly conducive to community building. The more they interacted with Swiss society to fill these needs, the wider the cultural and religious exchanges became, and the deeper the cleavage.

The second development has to do with how family reunification spurred a rapid growth in the migrant population. According to the Bundesamt für Statistik (Swiss Federal Statistical Office, FSO), its decadal increase went from 16,353 in 1970 to 56,625 in 1980, mainly among Balkan and Turkish Muslims. By 1990 the Muslim population had more than doubled to 152,217, and it had doubled again by the year 2000 to 310,807 (of whom 176,100 were Balkan).

Table 1 below gives a general breakdown of the Muslim population from 1970 to 2000.

Table 1 General population of Muslims in Switzerland

Year	Men	%	Women	%	Growth	Citizens	Age Group	
1970	11,036	67.5	5,317	32.5	16,353	456	≤ 15 yrs	91,948
1980	35,891	63.4	20,734	36.6	56,625	2,941	15–24 yrs	59,867
1990	96,783	63.6	55,434	36.4	152,217	7,735	25–39 yrs	91,436
2000	169,726	54.6	141,081	45.4	310,807	36,481	40–59 yrs	59,707
							≥ 60 yrs	7,849

Source: Swiss Federal Statistical Office (FSO)

Besides guest workers, political-asylum seekers, and economic refugees, this table also includes second-generation children and third-generation grandchildren born in Switzerland. If the first generation saw itself as part of an ethnic minority, these young people—now receiving Swiss education—did not necessarily view ethnicity as the central feature of their identity. Indeed, they carried multiple identities. In a sense, they had become both Muslim *and* Swiss, not unlike the native Swiss who converted to Islam. Swiss Muslims are relatively young: half are under the age of twenty-five. Some Muslim migrants also acquired citizenship through marriage with Swiss citizens. Finally, the table overall indicates double the number of men as women in the seventies. As the decades wore on, the ratio began to equalize.

Although Islam, as I have argued before, is not new to Europe, what is new is the speed and diversity with which the influx of migrants has transformed the Muslim presence in the postwar period. The big question is how Muslims who have settled permanently in Switzerland will be able to meet the basic needs of their community. More specifically, how long will they content themselves with prayer halls in place of mosques?

The refusal to grant them the full rights of citizenry can only encourage defensive mechanisms to preserve whatever traditions they know best, be they imported or not, religious or ethnic. For one thing, the majority of Muslims in Europe will continue to prefer marriage within their own ethnicities.

Swiss Muslims in closer focus

After discussing the broader demographic origins of the Swiss Muslim community, I want to offer a clearer breakdown according to socioeconomic, religious, and political indicators.

A 2010 report called *"Muslime in der Schweiz"* ("Muslims in Switzerland") for the Eidgenössische Kommission für

Migrationsfragen (EKM, the Swiss Commission for Migration), describes the present reality of ethnic diversity among Muslims thus:

Muslims in Switzerland feature, just like members of other religious communities, a very heterogeneous profile. Like the predominant part of the members of Christian denominations and other religions, the vast majority of the members of Muslim communities are secularly oriented. They understand themselves as citizens of this country, work in various professions, have diverse national backgrounds and cultural traditions, and belong to different social layers. The commitment of Islam takes different forms, and associated religious practices show a wide range of individual forms[76] [*my translation*].

Swiss Muslims are divided along national, cultural, social class, and ritualistic lines. The same type of heterogeneity exists among Christians and other religions. Here is how EKM describes Muslims with respect to nationality for 2000.

Table 2: Origin of Muslim population of Switzerland

Regions and Countries		Quantity
Balkan	Yugoslavia	108,058
	Bosnia-Herzegovina	23,457
	Macedonia	43,365
	Croatia	392
	Slovenia	102

---

76   Matteo Gianni et al., "Muslime in der Schweiz: Identitätsprofile, Erwartungen und Einstellungen," Eine Studie der Forschungsgruppe «Islam in der Schweiz» (GRIS), Hrg. von Eidgenössische Kommission für Migrationsfragen EKM, Zweite Auflage, 2010, BBL, Bundespublikationen, Bern.

Regions and Countries		Quantity
	Albania	699
Turkey		62,698
West Asia and North Africa	Morocco	4,364
	Tunisia	3,318
	Algeria	2,654
	Egypt	865
	Libya	489
	Iraq	3,171
	Lebanon	1,277
	Syria	459
	Palestine	156
Africa countries of southern Sahara	Senegal	562
	Sierra Leone	304
	Ethiopia	250
	Somalia	3,655
Iran		2,039
Central Asia	Afghanistan	1,831
South and Southeast Asia	Pakistan	1,681
	Bangladesh	648
	India	151
	Indonesia	331
Swiss		36,481

Source: Swiss Federal Statistical Office (FSO)

In this table, which reveals only the bare outlines of the existing diversity based on nationality, Balkan Muslims clearly take the lead, followed by Turks and Arabs, respectively. Two implications flow from this fact. First, Switzerland is home to Muslims mostly of indisputably native *European* origin— mainly Bosnian, Croatian, Slovenian, and Turkish. They are all native to Europe. Second, Switzerland is home to Muslims who come from Muslim-majority countries—namely, Morocco, Egypt, Iran, Somalia, Pakistan, and Indonesia.[77]

---

77 The term *Islamic countries* refers here to countries with Muslim majorities, including the "Arab countries."

As sources of the Swiss Federal Statistical Office (FSO) demonstrate, I would like to highlight a further point, namely, that about half of the 36,481 called "Swiss Muslims" are native converts to Islam, distinct from second- and third-generation migrants who are born in Switzerland.

Let us now look at the geographic dispersion of Switzerland's Muslim population. Table 3, from an EKM research report for 2000, gives an overview of the Muslim population in all twenty-six cantons of Switzerland.

The majority of Muslims live in large urban cantons such as Zürich, Bern, St. Gallen, Aargau, Vaud, and Geneva, whereas 18.7 percent of native Swiss Muslims are found in the western French-speaking rather than German-speaking part and in the rural regions (e.g., Graubünden 9.25 percent, Uri 11.5 percent, Zug 11.6 percent, and Jura 15.6 percent).

The EKM research group on the Muslims in Switzerland has raised an interesting, still unanswered question about whether the strong difference between these two linguistic regions can be explained in terms of culture and mentality. Although I do not think I have found an answer yet, Switzerland nevertheless has no real ghettos compared with other Western countries— no *banlieux* on the scale of Marseille or Bradford.

Some people contend that Bümpliz and Bethlehem, suburbs of the capital, Bern, are basically ghettos. In France two-thirds of Les Rosiers, a suburb of Marseille, is of Arab origin, which makes the native French segment a minority. A similar situation where natives are in the minority exists in Bradford, England. But the same is not true of either Bümpliz or Bethlehem. According to the 2008 *Statistisches Jahrbuch der Stadt Bern* (Statistical Yearbook of the City of Bern), Swiss citizens in Bümpliz and Bethlehem made up 11,398 out of a total population of 15,781 and 8,242 out of 12,693, respectively. Bümpliz and Bethlehem belong to Bern's *Stadtteil VI*, or sixth

Table 3: Muslim population in the Swiss Cantons

Canton	Muslims per Canton	in %	Swiss Muslims	in %
Zürich	66,520	5.3	9,519	14.3
Bern	28,377	2.9	3,083	10.8
Luzern	13,227	3.8	1,346	10.1
Uri	683	1.9	79	11.5
Schwyz	5,598	4.3	227	4
Obwalden	985	3	77	7.8
Nidwalden	812	2.2	96	11.8
Glarus	2,480	6.5	95	3.8
Zug	4,248	4.2	495	11.6
Solothurn	13,165	5.4	815	6.1
Basel Stadt	12,643	6.7	1,446	11.4
Basel Land	11,053	4.2	1,055	9.5
Schaffhausen	4,254	5.8	396	9.3
Appenzell Ausserrhoden	1,528	2.8	116	7.5
Appenzell Innerrhoden	503	3.4	16	3.1
St. Gallen	27,747	6.1	1,598	5.7
Graubünden	3,913	2.1	362	9.25
Aargau	30,072	4.5	2,144	7.1
Thurgau	13,584	5.9	836	6.1
Freiburg	7,389	3	1,108	15
Vaud	24,757	3.9	3,628	14.7
Wallis	7,394	2.7	714	9.6
Neuchâtel	5,056	3	921	18.2
Geneva	17,762	4.3	5,338	30
Jura	1,310	1.9	205	15.6
Ticino	5,747	1.9	764	13.3
General total	**310,807**	**4.3**	**36,481**	**11.75**
Western Switzerland	**63,668**	**3.5**	**11,914**	**18.7**
German part of Switzerland	**241,392**	**4.6**	**23,803**	**9.8**

Source: Swiss Federal Statistical Office (FSO)

district. Of their total combined population of 28,474, therefore, 31 percent are foreigners, and still a higher percentage are Europeans native to Germany, Spain, Portugal, and so on. People of Turkish origin total only 615, Kosovars 593.

Although high-rise apartment blocks do exist, they are not comparable to those in France, the United Kingdom, or Germany. In Bümpliz and, especially, Bethlehem skyscrapers are rented mostly by foreigners. People from the Balkans live in apartment blocks, where they are able to nurture their traditions through religious and cultural upbringing, cooking styles, and satellite and cable television from their homelands.

Muslim institutions and organizations

Approximately 50 organizations and 130 cultural centers and prayer places underpin the ethnicity or nationality of Swiss Muslims (26 Arab, 49 Albanian, 21 Bosnian, and 31 Turkish). However, it should be noted that Swiss Muslims do not organize themselves based only on religion. Indeed, cultural bonds seem even stronger than religious ones.

Alone the names of the various organizations indicate that the associations orient themselves more on cultural and social (for example, the nationalities) than on purely religious criteria.[78] [*my translation*]

The names given to many of these organizations, cultural centers, and even mosques demonstrate the importance attached to culture—e.g., Türkische Moschee (a Turkish mosque in Werrikon), Albanische Moschee (an Albanian mosque in Zofingen), and Bosnischer Kulturverein (a Bosnian cultural association in Rheineck).

In Switzerland, unlike other Western countries, *Moscheen* (mosques) are rudimentary structures styled on *Hinterhöfen, Garagen, und Lagerhäusen* (backyards, garages, and warehouses),

78   Gianni, "Muslime in der Schweiz," 23.

which Muslims are no longer permitted to decorate with minarets. Farhad Afshar has called this situation *kulturellen Niemandsland* (a cultural no-man's-land), where Islam has not been openly and rightly recognized as a public religion.[79]

Not only are nationality and language a major element in the statistical breakdown, but so are differences in the way Islam is practiced and understood. This is easily observable through women's dress. Yemeni women cover themselves in such a way as to leave no bare skin, and sometimes their eyes too. An Albanian mother may fully cover her hair with a headscarf, whereas her daughter chooses to wear makeup openly. By the same token, Iranian women tend to arrange their headscarves so that the front part of the hair is left exposed.

Women occupy a telling place in the dynamics now at play. As Georgetown University Professor Yvonne Haddad puts it, "women have sort of become the banner of Islam." It is true on both sides. Of all the topics debated about Muslims in the West, the hijāb, niqāb, and burka rank at the top. After successfully banning minaret construction, the Swiss are contemplating a ban on headscarves at school and the burka in public places. Other issues affecting Muslims are the search for a separate *Muslime Friedhofe* (Muslim cemetery),[80] halāl meat, and proper training courses for imams. Cities such as Bern, Geneva, and Zürich have Muslim graveyards, and Turkish and Albanian butcheries dot the country selling *Halāl-Fleisch*. However, Switzerland forbids the private slaughter of animals.

Which leaves one of the most important issues: the training of imams. It is important because training imams within the secular and direct-democratic context of Switzerland is healthier

79   René Pahud De Mortages and Erwin Tanner, Hrsg. *Muslime und schweizerische Rechtsordnung / Les musulmans et l'ordre juridique suisse*, Freiburger Veröffentlichungen zum Religionsrecht (FVRR), Bd. 13, (Freiburg: Schulthess, 2002), p. 190.
80   Part of a Muslim ritual is to wrap the dead with white material in place of a casket and then to position the body so that it faces the Kaabah, the most sacred building which is in Mecca, Saudi Arabia.

than parachuting them from abroad with next to no knowledge of the local context. Western-educated imams can play a major role in reconciling the best values of Islam with the best of the West. To make Islam an integral part of Western society, they are best placed to redefine Muslim identity within a Western context. This is the challenge from which Switzerland cannot afford to flinch.

- 8 -
Caught in the Crossfire

"*NDOVU WAWILI WAKIPIGANA, ZIUMIAZO ni nyasi*," goes a Swahili proverb—"When two elephants fight, it is the grass that suffers." It comes to mind every time I witness a conflict where each party seems oblivious to the consequences. When parents abuse each other, are they always aware of the adverse effect on their children?

Magnify this many times and you will get an idea of the damage that conflict on the scale envisaged by Huntington would truly look like if his predictions came true. Our world is already rife with conflicts waged more or less at the cost of untold innocent lives. The global war on terrorism is a prime example. The rights of civilians are routinely trampled on by the elephants of terrorism and counterterrorism. But it would be much worse if the main actors were "civilizations," in Huntington's sense.

Two to tango

In Switzerland, the peaceful mainstream of Islam has been caught in the crossfire for far too long. But crossfire between which two parties? Certain political forces in the country have successfully generalized and manipulated sentiments of fear and insecurity among the public. These sentiments have heightened to a point where a selective response to danger has become more difficult. Although the result of the 2009 referendum surprised many Swiss, the truth is that a 57.5 percent majority approved the blanket, indiscriminate ban on all minarets. What started as a right-wing demand snowballed into a law that has inflicted a deep scar on interfaith relations across Switzerland. During a previous campaign of the SVP denouncing the naturalization of migrants, placards could be seen on which migrants were associated with Osama bin Laden. Muslims were terrorists, and the Swiss, they argued, were best forewarned about accepting them as full citizens in their midst.

In point of fact, such virulent Islamophobic campaigns were directed not only at Muslims, but at all *Ausländern* (foreigners), and there is nothing new in that. The *corps d'élite* of the right-wing Swiss People's Party has a well-earned reputation for overtly racist campaigns. In 2007, the UN complained about a racist propaganda poster, just as it did during their 2009 ban campaign. The poster in question, advocating the deportation of foreigners, showed three white sheep kicking a black sheep out of the Swiss flag. Such is the extremist tone of Europe's ultraconservative political currents nowadays. Aliens are aliens—no exceptions, not even Switzerland's neighbors, with whom they share values.

The European "debate" on foreigners has spawned all kinds of right-wing terms: even Switzerland's neighbors, the Germans and Italians, feel the fire. The term *Überfremdung* (foreign infiltration) has come into currency warning the *Germanisierung* of Swiss universities (that is, there are too many students from Germany). Italian compatriots are simply *Tschingg* (equivalent to *niggers?*). And now merely saying *Muslimen* has a disturbingly pejorative ring to it in the West just as *die Deutsche* (the Germans) does in Switzerland.

Big Brother

This atmosphere has had a psychological effect on the minds of foreigners in general and Muslims in particular. Today Muslims feel uncomfortable even inside their mosques. I have personally heard a Friday sermon in Bern in which an imam referred to the presence of spies in mosques. The mutual suspicion is as tragic as it is palpable. It tends to kill debate. I myself was once called a spy because I invited fellow worshippers to a public lecture titled "Islamic Family Law Contested."[81]

Do Muslims—or other human beings, for that matter—deserve to live in an Orwellian nightmare where "Big Brother is watching you," where even the most decent motives are suspect?

It is not just the spying that troubles everyone, but the accusatory finger that never lets up, a sentiment especially felt by asylum seekers. Having little contact with Swiss society and very insecure in their new environment, they feel trapped and powerless to defend themselves even against false accusations. How would you feel if you had just escaped the Assad dictatorship, only to face new hardship wrought by right-wing extremists?

---

81   In 2006, while studying at the University of Bern, I attended a semester-long lecture on Islamic family law at the Institute of Islamic Studies and Social Anthropology. The institute then organized a ten-day workshop titled "Islamisches Familenrecht im Wandel," which ended with a public lecture and debate. I brought a poster to the mosque. But the word *Wandel* (transition, or development) angered some Muslims, who insisted, "Islam doesn't change, Shari'ah doesn't change." Ironically, it was a young Egyptian imam who, having attended the events, agreed to hang the poster inside the locked glass-window board. A few left the premises, angrily banging the door behind them. Dr. Nahda Shehada of the Institute of Social Studies delivered a public lecture. Three Muslim scholars participated in the workshops and debate: Sheikh Taysir Bayyud al-Tamimi (Supreme Judge of Sharia Courts in Palestine), Sheikh Muhammad Jamal Abu Snayna (Qadi of Jerusalem), and Sheikh Ismail Abdulkader (Qadi of Tuareg-Imamate of Azawagh, Niger).

Muslims generally see Switzerland as a country so conservative, it will not hesitate to suppress the freedom of religion for the most arcane reasons. Some right-wing placards in the canton of Aargau incited fellow Swiss to refuse to turn Baden into Baghdad. They showed the uncovered, smiling face of a fair-skinned woman alongside another fully covered with a burka. Between them the slogan read *"Maria statt Schariah"* (Maria instead of Shari'ah). The suggestion is that Muslims are bent on destroying the true values of Swiss Maria to make way for the Swiss Shari'ah, the tone clearly designed to set the stage for the "debate" on banning burkas. In a single stroke ultraconservatives, not famed for their solidarity with feminist causes, have taken up the fight for "women's equal rights" as well as the "safety" of the Swiss. And they do not give two hoots how much racism or Islamophobia they fan through their scare tactics. Wearing the burka simply equals turning Baden into Baghdad, liberal values into a Shari'ah state. Minarets are missiles aimed against Switzerland; they are part of the Muslim invasion.

Is ignorance an excuse?

Anti-Muslim propaganda has worked well because most Swiss have almost no understanding of Islam or acquaintance with the Muslims living among them. Nor could they be bothered to ask themselves if Muslims really want to establish a Shari'ah State of Switzerland modeled on some marginal strain of fundamentalists elsewhere. Even if that were true, the fear would have been comprehensible if the country were at least minimally anchored in Christianity. But religion is not really at issue here, any more than it is in the rest of Europe; rather it is a matter of perceptions.

People in positions of power, who perhaps should know better, have created an intolerable level of suspicion and hatred against "outsiders." Is Swiss secularism so fragile that it might soon be trampled underfoot by a community of 400,000

Muslims? Something really has to be done if Switzerland is to preserve its standing among civilized nations as a defender of liberty. If mosques with minarets do not undermine secular states—at least not on this planet—then a whole mind-set clearly has to change. Rational debate cannot take root in the interstellar space that separates the two sides. Without middle-ground agreement that each side must commit itself to peaceful coexistence, what is the purpose of debate? If one side or the other does not aspire to coherent relations among the country's many communities, then why not just give in and let nihilism, extremism, and all the ills of the last century lead the way again?

Muslims have their work cut out for them

Muslims have many challenges to overcome, and the most important have to be met within their own ranks. If anything, they should ask themselves how long their mosques should remain financially dependent on aid from Aurupa Milli Görüs Teskilatlan (Turkey), the Muslim World League (Saudi Arabia), and the Muslim Brotherhood (Egypt). Why not wean themselves away from reliance on "exported" imams?

And why not lead by example in the search for peaceful coexistence? What could be better than that, if they indeed wish to find their true place in Swiss society? They have nothing to fear, because they still enjoy a large reservoir of support among the native Swiss. This was obvious during the minaret-ban campaign. The Swiss Federal Council (*der Bundesrat*), parliament, fifteen of eighteen political parties (including Christian), concerned associations, and organizations around the country (including Christian) recommended voting against the initiative.[82]

Already in 1992, Reinhard Schulze wrote that Westerners

---

82 See http://www.parlament.ch.

considered *Islam* a synonym for *terror.*[83] The "clash" debate will flare up again and again not only because ultraconservatives preach the Islamic Threat, but also because Muslims feel too insecure in Western Europe to take a determined stance on internal reform. But Europe and America are their new homes.

I once heard a young woman telling CNN how she answered people in the United States when they claimed that what she wore looked foreign, that Americans did not wear hijāb or niqāb. "I'm from the nation's capital, lady," she said. "I'm sorry to put it that way, but please stop telling me we don't do that here, because I'm from here, and I am here. My family's raised here. I live here … You might not do it here, but I do it here."[84]

What she meant, of course, was that Islam is a reality in the West. Islam is no longer a religion of *Ausländern* (foreigners).

83   Michael Lüder, Hg., *Der Islam im Aufbruch? Perspektiven der arabischen Welt*, Serie Piper Band, (München: Piper, 1992), 94.
84   CNN documentary "Muslim Women Who Cover in America." Two Muslim American women wearing hijāb (Aliya) and niqāb (Nadia) spoke about their choice to cover themselves in adherence to their faith, plus the social consequences they face. The above quotation is from twenty-five-year-old Nadia. She is speaking as an African-American born and raised in the United States.

- 9 -
Toward a Helvetius Muslim Identity

THERE IS NO DOUBT that Europe's demographic changes have thrown up new and unfamiliar challenges before which Europeans—both Muslim and non-Muslims—face two fateful choices: make Muslims part of the policy solutions or keep excluding them. The clash of civilizations may be only a theory with little or no historical basis, but the thin arguments it uses has features that are alluring to the crowd. It is incumbent upon our generation to seek practical solutions, rather than insist on the narrative of one insular side or the other.

Ethnocentrism is no solution at all; it is a recipe for worse crises.

A realistic assessment of the Swiss context will show that solutions are indeed possible. But transcending conflicts requires the active participation of everyone concerned within not only a civil, but a sustained dialogue complemented by as many separate discussions on specific problems and their solutions as the country needs.

As healthy as this vision may be, each community still has the responsibility to sort out its internal confusion or disorientation with a view to rechanneling its energies beyond its boundaries and engaging other communities. Fruitful external dialogue, in large part, rests on the fruits of internal dialogue. I am thinking here of the community I know best. There is a pressing need for Muslims to engage in internal dialogue, before any other dialogue. Moreover, they must look to its success rather than accept the sterility of an endless rehashing of issues. Ultimately, they have to plot the steps toward a new Swiss identity.

The justice of honesty

It is not a simple question of finding solutions. Muslims must also ask about the character of these solutions, because this will allow them also to define the perimeters within which Muslims and non-Muslims will be able to draw mutual profit from their dialogue. In this spirit the solutions must be reasonable and just. I have never argued that Switzerland should be an Islamic country, but neither are Muslims obligated to adopt everything with a "Swiss" label, good or bad. Islam has no need to justify itself. It is as much a world religion as Christianity; no amount of defamation can alter this fact.

Therefore, both religions must be respected, the participation of all concerned encouraged.

Beyond the internal perimeters of where Muslims would like to take the debate, I believe conditions should be placed for a truly legitimate, mutually enriching debate.

The first condition requires that Islam not be put in question or its recognition fought every inch of the way.

The second is that Muslims—who, as we saw, already recognize Christians as "People of the Book," just like them— should consider how to make Helvetius part of their identity.

If we genuinely seek dialogue, then we need to ask two things. One, which Islamic and Swiss values are we referring to as we explore the norms of citizenship shared by all the Swiss people?

Two, in which context?

Is it worth the effort to dialogue with Muslims of every variety?

I do not think this is possible or necessary. Muslims differ according to religious tradition and country of origin, but they also feel at home with fellow Muslims with whom they have little in common besides the *ummah* (community in Islam) and the basic tenets of the faith. This fellowship becomes more problematic with Salafis militants such as Hizb ut-Tahrir. Dialoguing with Islamic militants, even those who are not violent, is difficult in the best of times, because it is not always clear that they consider their opponents Muslim at all. Sufis, on the other hand, are often the exact opposite.

But Muslims differ in other ways, too. In tolerant societies they tend to hold more open views on a gamut of issues than those who have to struggle under severe conditions, as in Switzerland. British Muslims are far more likely to have professional occupations, management positions, or their own businesses than their counterparts in Switzerland. Are the British a lot more accepting of their Muslim neighbors than the Swiss? It would be unthinkable for them to outlaw fundamental rights of religious expression. Despite their dire need, Swiss Muslims have no more than a handful of mosques in which to worship.

As Adonis put it, there is more than one type of Islam, and Europe is not homogenous.[85] A federal republic, Switzerland exhibits two characteristics especially relevant to my discussion: direct democracy and cultural diversity. It is home to four official languages; its citizens have the power to overturn parliamentary decisions by submitting any constitutional initiative or referendum they desire. More broadly, a correct appreciation of the character of differences within each party to the dialogue I propose would spare everyone a lot of frustration

---

85   Khalid Al-Maaly, Hg., *Die Arabische Welt: Zwischen Tradition und Moderne* (Heidelberg: Palmyra Verlag, 2004), 54.

and disappointment. Internal differences by themselves should not ruin the dialogue, which has to start somewhere.

Conflict worker approach to the current "conflict"

I want to use Johan Galtung's model of conflict transformation, based on "diagnosis, prognosis and therapy," to transform crisis between Muslims and conservatives in Switzerland:

1. *Right-wing parties*, who claim that Muslims have no intention of integrating, that they force their daughters to wear the hijab and into arranged marriages, and that Islam is inherently violent and incompatible with Western values. *Überfremdung* (foreign infiltration) poses a danger, which they illustrate with a prediction that it will turn the city of Baden (in the canton of Aargau), among others, into Baghdad, where women walk around in burkas. Switzerland's "Maria values" must not be replaced by those of the Shari'ah. No Islamization in Switzerland, no minarets.

2. *The Muslim community at large*, which sees Switzerland as a conservative country where right-wing politicians can freely advocate for more, not less, discrimination against targeted groups of people. Although few of them force their daughters either to don the hijab or to enter into marriages against their will, mainstream Muslims sense that their freedom of religion has been suppressed because of those among them who may hold marginal religious views.

The two main traits of behavior in this "face-off" are as follows:

1. *Right-wingers react to the Muslim presence* with fearmongering about a takeover of the country by Islam and about specific public issues such as minarets, which they portray as Islamic power aimed at the heart of their country.

2. *Muslims respond to right-wing fearmongering* by retreating into their ghettolike communities, complaining about discrimination, and participating in demonstrations.

Conflict worker: All Muslims are targeted. Therefore, on the one side stands the entire mainstream community of Muslims, who exercise little influence in Swiss politics, and on the other are the right-wing Swiss extremists leading the demand for exclusionary measures. The latter's referendum campaign leads to a law banning minarets outright.

Referenda can be deceiving. They often give the illusion that something of great import has been solved. The reality is that the underlying problem in the case of post-referendum Switzerland—namely, integration—remains untouched. Indeed, the referendum has merely postponed the matter, though not without hurting and humiliating law-abiding Muslims. One reaction of the latter has been to assume a more passive public posture, even though it would be perfectly normal for them to play their hand again and win. Conceivably, Muslims could avail themselves of direct democracy and call a referendum of their own that challenges the banning law. After all, this is the name of the game in Swiss direct democracy.

If only "winning" diminished the Islamophobia and the daily discrimination they face. Winning a onetime contest such as a referendum alone is not a solution that can *transcend* and *transform* the ongoing conflict in a positive direction. Besides, a "transcending solution" aims for a win-win, not winner-loser, objective. But if we accept that "transcendence" offers the best prospect for conflict transformation, the key then becomes dialogue in all its forms, both public and private.

Such a dialogue has to generate the creative ideas necessary to attract large, representative segments from both communities, Muslim and non-Muslim. Each party has to want to preserve the legitimate interests of two *communities,* rather than to advocate for the interests of a political grouping claiming to speak on behalf of one community against the other. It is neither right nor fair to ask one community to bend to the vision of any given grouping with a political agenda.

No doubt, Muslim and non-Muslim would harbor the same suspicions about each other even without their respective extremists venting those suspicions in public. Through dialogue, however, they can safeguard against religiously or politically motivated violence without undermining the full rights of the citizenry.

The attainment of social peace is tantalizingly within reach, because in the end both Muslims and non-Muslims concur in their peaceful ends. For Muslims, peace is part of their faith because *Islam* literally means "peace" and requires them to privilege the peaceful resolution of conflict. And non-Muslims desire the sociopolitical peace they have enjoyed even through two world wars.

Who would not desire peace for the society in which they live, raise their families, and educate themselves? But it will take both communities acting as productive sources for peaceful resolutions.

As far as I can tell, there is one major hindrance to this: Islam is still perceived as the problem. It is perceived this way, I believe, because Islam's detractors think they can interpret it with reference not to how Muslims actually live it but to how handfuls of violent conspirators have grouped together around a set of blatant distortions of Islam. Every religion has its "distorters"; why are only Muslims expected to be an exception to the rule? Non-Muslims need to understand better how Muslims live their Islam.

For this to happen, Muslims themselves need to clarify the abiding sources of Islam to their own rising generation, above all. Young people who suffer alienation from their society and from themselves should not have to seek a sense of belonging among those too willing to exploit their suffering.

Dialogue demands mutual respect, but mutual respect cannot take place without self-understanding, first, and then a proper understanding of what others believe, fear, and take inspiration from.

Swiss converts to Islam have the opportunity to play a key role in bridging the cultural gulf and acting as the agents of peace, so to speak. They can teach the rest of the population to put their suspicions aside and walk hand in hand with their neighbors. They can demonstrate how illusory the walls are. They are best placed to distinguish Islam from Arab, Turkish, or Somali culture. They are Muslim not because they want to become instant Arabs, but because they love Islam and the life that flows from their personal choices.

Equally important are second-, third-, and fourth-generation Muslims, who generally can handle local Swiss customs with more confidence than their forebears. By identifying themselves as *Swiss* Muslims, they can go a long way toward overcoming the internal differences besetting their community and thus speak with a new voice.

Every Muslim, no matter his or her origin, has to participate in the ongoing process to create a way of life that is more compatible with the European context. It is a challenge. But when faced without recklessly amplifying existing fears, it can diffuse the tension that has led to the imposition of what amounts to punitive laws upon the Muslims of Switzerland, laws that are completely counterproductive in the effort toward fuller integration.

There is an ethno-cultural dimension to the ongoing

tensions in Swiss society, and Muslims have to come to grips with it better if they are to bring the various viewpoints in their midst into sync. Self-understanding is one of the prerequisites to a healthy dialogue.

After that, what reason would anyone have to demand that Muslim rights be curtailed in the interest of "national security"? There are more important issues to think about than the erection of minarets.

How can we become the victors of peace instead of the victims of conflict? This is what we should all be demanding of each other, Muslims and people of other faiths as well as those of no faith.

PART IV
A Way Forward

- 10 -
Elements of Internal Muslim Dialogue

I SLAM TRACES ITS ROOTS to Abraham. He lived in Mecca, which Prophet Muhammad reclaimed as part of the long tradition passed down without interruption to what we know as the Islamic era. Therefore, it was inevitable that Islamic practice should take on the local colors and culture of the place where "Islam," in this elementary sense, reflowered—the Arab Peninsula.

Not surprisingly, the Arabian flowering left a deep imprint on Islam's subsequent development. However, what started out as an important cultural synthesis capable of adapting to new environments around the world has come to be identified with Islam itself by some who, in their effort to recover the authentic roots of Islam, came to reject its richness and variety. In doing so, they reject the history and accomplishments of Islam. You see, it is not only Muslims' ignorant of Islam who identify Islam with Arabs; many Arab and non-Arab Muslims have come to believe this, even though without non-Arabs—who constitute the vast majority of Muslims—Islam would be unrecognizable today.

Ultimately, though, *any* specific culture—not just the Arab tradition—may pose serious obstacles to further development and be counterproductive in the face of modern challenges. The truth is that Islam is neither an Arab nor a tribal religion. And yet the Arab dress code holds pride of place for many devout Muslims around the world. Muslims in East Africa mistake the traditional Arab dresses they wear—such as the *thawb* and *hebaya*—for "Islamic" clothing. They do it for various reasons, not the least of which is a need to distinguish themselves and to belong.

When this tendency is too strong, it becomes a hindrance to dealing with the challenges of the contemporary world.

Islam from essential sources to diversity

If Muslims are to escape being victims both of their cultures and of those who wish them ill, then they need to understand the core principles of their faith and how these principles give rise to cultural expression.[86] The fact that they share these core principles but not any single overarching culture demonstrates that culture is subordinate to their faith. Each culture simply reflects the manner in which they have applied their core principles and collectively adapted to specific environments generation after generation.

Muslims take guidance from two chief sources: the Holy Qur'ān and the Sunnah (the body of Islamic custom and practice based on the words and deeds of the Prophet Muhammad). But Islamic practice and ritual do not end here. From these two sources several highly developed traditions have evolved into

---

86   People can be victims *of* their own cultures. For example, many women suffer the custom of genital mutilation. People can be victimized also *for* their culture. Unlike the former situation, where people of the same culture toture against each other in the name of their own customs, the latter refers to one culture victimizing other people of different culture due to differences.

full-fledged schools embracing law, theology, and mysticism.[87] Though they agree on the essentials of their faith, Muslims enjoy considerable leeway in interpretation and specific practices, which include everything from "temporary marriage" to matters relating to dogma. Some follow in the footsteps of the great mystics, whose shrines they have preserved. With respect to nonobligatory rituals, others make use of music and dancing, praise the virtues of "spiritual wine," or fast seven days of Ramadan (as do the Alevis) instead of the conventional thirty days.

These particularities combine with other factors to distinguish Muslims of Arab, Albanian, African, and Balkan descents from each other. A Saudi Arab is neither a Yemeni nor an African Arab. In a country of recent immigration such as Switzerland, Muslims have congregated from every corner of the world for a better life, bringing with them distinctive cultural features. Most prayer houses in Switzerland (usually in garages and industrial buildings) serve specific ethnic groups (Alban, Arabic, Tamil, Turkish, and so on). If Muslims are united by the witness they bear to the oneness of Allah and his messenger Muhammad, they are also distinguishable by their ethnicity and the way they apply the teachings of their respective schools of jurisprudence.

---

87 Khalid Al-Maaly, *Die Arabische Welt: Zwischen Tradition und Modern*, p. 81. I am using *schools* here in a much broader sense than that of the five recognized *madhahib* or jurisprudential traditions—namely, Maliki, Hanafi, Shafi'i, Hanbali, and Ja'fari.

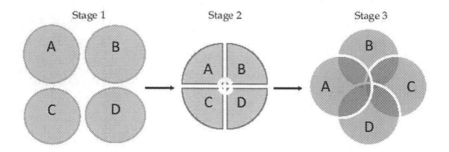

Diagram 2 The Ummah-Toolkit (UT) of The Point of Universal Principles of Islam (PUPI).

The diagram above illustrates the diversity, unity, and unity in diversity that exists among Muslims living in the Western world. Each circle represents an ethnicity. Thus, A may represent Albanians, B Berbers, C Turks, and D Nubians. The first part of the diagram (far left) indicates Muslims living in separate ethnic spaces, where ethnic or national identity is the defining characteristic. An African-American will call himself Mohammed, a Bedouin Muhammad, a Turk Mehmet, a Fulani Mamadu, and a Bajun Madi. And yet they are all Muslim. Although they have the same name as the Prophet, they illustrate a particular localized version of that name. Incidentally, when they refer to the Prophet, they will pronounce his name in the original Arabic.

In Switzerland mosques typically cater to specific ethnicities. There are Albanian mosques, Arab mosques, Turkish mosques, and so on. Therefore, an Albanian mosque will have an Albanian imam to lead prayers, and its sermons will be in the Albanian language. Likewise with Arab and Turkish mosques. I should mention that although the identity of each mosque is unmistakable, other Muslims are not barred. With all their differences, Muslims continue to enjoy a sense of community that is perhaps unique among the world traditions. They not only perceive and recognize, but also encompass, their differences. Brotherhood and sisterhood run across ethnic lines. This is portrayed in the diagram above as the second stage.

This explains why the *ummah* (community in Islam) has not lost its significance through the centuries. As a concept it is central to what it means to be a Muslim. When Muslims bear witness (in Arabic: *shahāda*) to the Oneness of God (in Arabic: Allah) and Muhammad as the Prophet of God, they stand together. The most striking evidence for the abiding reality of the ummah's spiritual unity is the hajj to Mecca. The largest in the world, this annual pilgrimage symbolizes Muslims coming together from every corner of the world to take part in ritual dress. Malcolm X (El-Hajj Malik El-Shabazz) said it best in his autobiography: "[N]ever have I witnessed such sincere hospitality." To him the hajj had an overwhelming "spirit of true brotherhood" where people of all colors and races meet.[88]

The ummah model is indicated by the second stage of the diagram. Muslims here are more conscious of themselves as a single community. This is clearly observable in the Muslim response to the plight of the Palestinians. Africans at one time united to help South Africans defeat the apartheid regime. Just as South African freedom was African freedom, so Palestinian freedom is the freedom of all Muslims. Despite their differences, Muslims are united around the liberation of the Palestinian people, because Palestinians are part of the ummah.

This second stage in the diagram above is a split circle. As people of the same faith Muslims are a unit, but here this does not detract from the particularities they celebrate (language, clothes, food, customs, nationalities, and so on). What they miss is a critical approach to the ummah as a unity in difference (third stage), where no single cultural identity need be idealized for all times and in every place. A genuine

88   Alex Haley, *Autobiography of Malcolm X* (New Jersey: Research & Education Association, 1996), p. 73.

understanding of the fundamental principles of Islam would be enough to affirm what is best in each local culture.

That is what the third stage demonstrates. The point of this exercise is to see how European Muslims can build their future in the soil of *their* national cultures, not according to some false cultural ideal disembodied from its original setting. They certainly need not be Arabized to be Muslims.

Unlike the first stage, where circles (ethnic groups) are separate from one another, and the second stage with ethnicities brought together as a single group, in this final stage groups exhibit ethnic differences upon encountering one another. The point at which they intersect is almost like a "melting pot," in which all cultures blend together into the larger Islamic identity. I call this the Point of Universal Principles of Islam (PUPI).

PUPI is a different way of thinking about the ummah. Rather than artificial unity, it consciously sees and appreciates diversity with the knowledge that at some point *all Muslims are united by the universal principles of Islam*. PUPI is somewhat present in the second stage, as we see in the diagram, but it is more visible in this third stage, where consciousness comes into play as the debate gains importance.

Throughout this process, debate, discussion, and dialogue are critical to putting the concept of a global Muslim community, a modern ummah, into practice. However, the process reaches its apogee when Islam is delinked from its extraneous cultural expressions and reaffirms the global, transnational, and universally shared set of patterns that make up the Islamic identity.[89]

Thanks to their awareness of the fundamental principles of Islam, in this last stage Muslims adopt and consciously celebrate unity in diversity. It is here that Western Muslims

---

89 Roy, *Globalised Islam*, p. 120.

can prepare, always through dialogue, to act within a context of diversity and social pluralism.

PUPI in practice

The Point of Universal Principles of Islam is integral to any broad internal dialogue across ethnic boundaries. One area where this can work is congregational prayer. As we saw, Muslims agree that *salāt* (prayer) is obligatory and, to most, that it consists of five prayers a day. However, they differ on the performance of this ritual, depending on their *madh'hab* (schools of jurisprudence). While standing, some Muslims hold the left wrist with the right hand beneath the chest, others beneath the navel; Malikīs and Ja'faris do not put their hands together at all.

In Switzerland, some mosques are attended by people of more than fifty nationalities. Some prime examples are the *Islamisches Zentrum Bern* (Islamic Center of Bern) in Lindenrain and *Islamische König Faysal Stiftung* (King Faisal Islamic Foundation) in Friedensgasse, Basel.[90] And yet they stand in one line, shoulder to shoulder, Kenyan Swahili next to Kurdish Turk, Malay next to Chechnyan. The Hausa or Fulani of Cameroon, wearing a colorful *agwada* dress, pray with their hands hanging at their sides; a Pashtun dresses in a white *piran tonbad,* and a Moroccan in a green *jelaba* with the right hand grasping the left hand placed below the chest. Likewise there are differences among the women. Some wear jeans, others skirts, and their hair stays covered or uncovered.

Which of the above is the true Muslim?

Viewing the outward variations of dress and prayer through the prism of the Universal Principles of Islam is crucially important for Muslims in the diaspora. They want to belong to the ummah, just like other Muslims, but to achieve this in concrete terms they need to exercise their critical faculties and

---

90   I have experience at the mosque in Bern since 2000 and about two years with the one in Basel.

power of judgment. They have to be *reflective* believers rather than mere believers. Falling back on blind tradition all the time will only deepen the rifts among them. They have to figure out how they should practice Islam where they live, not where their ancestors once lived.

So, let the Egyptian worshipper wonder about how the Indian Muslim beside him is praying. It is healthy. For a while, each may choose to believe that he or she is practicing the "right" Islam, but the big question will remain as long as there are human beings on earth: what indeed is the right way to practice Islam? No Muslims can properly answer this without reference to specific context and circumstances.

Muslims have to reflect deeply on both their faith and why they practice it as they do. Therein lies the hope and, I strongly believe, the true essence of Islam. Faith in Islam does not require Muslims to lead unquestioning lives. On the contrary, Muslims are exhorted to exert themselves in reasoning and acting.

Let us take the concrete example of proper dress.

Muslims are required to cover their private parts (*awrah*)— all agree that it is *harām* (forbidden) to pray naked. Therefore, covering one's body does not directly pertain to color or style of clothing. What matters is that private parts are covered, not whether the worshipper does it with a green jelaba or blue agwada. Style of dress—along with myriad other issues I will not bother to mention here—lie outside the purview of the Point of Universal Principles of Islam, which has to do with purpose and direction. How one dresses modestly depends mostly on ethnic customs or personal habits, not the fundamental obligation to dress modestly.

As elementary as it sounds, the example of dress illustrates an important aspect of Islamic practice as it has developed under universal principles through the centuries. The act of standing (*qiyām*) during prayer differs little, even though it touches on obligatory prayer. By reflecting on the obligation to pray from a universal vantage point, Muslims will gain a deeper understanding of the differences in how this obligation is carried out. Indeed, they would discover that the greatest imams in history, those who gave final form to how their followers ought to pray, accepted a certain degree of variation in prayer posture.

In short, there is no right or wrong way beyond standing upright and facing the *qiblah* (toward the Kaabah in Mecca). Moreover, those unable to stand upright because of illness or handicap need not stand at all; they may sit or lean against the wall. Why should someone who finds himself without clothes for a prolonged period of time be forbidden to pray? And if we follow the penetrating reasoning behind Islamic jurisprudence as it has developed through the centuries, the specific position of the hands becomes as optional as the style of dress. Neither defines or forms part of what I call the Universal Principles of Islam. A single obligatory aspect of prayer remains: to manifest one's intention of performing prayer according to ability.

- 11 -
From Multiple Views of Islam to Universal Islam

THE IDEA OF A "deculturalized" Islam at some initial stage, as I suggest in this book, is not new. Oliver Roy defines it as "a means of experiencing a religious identity that is not linked to a given culture and can therefore fit with every culture, or, more precisely, could be defined beyond the very notion of culture."[91]

Human beings view the world around them through different eyes. The "eyes" I am talking about are not a simple organ of vision, but a mental faculty steeped in social norms and mores through complex learning processes that begin in childhood. We gain our perceptions through a network of interactions—culture, education, beliefs, political views, and personal experiences—that helps us develop a worldview. Whether religious or secular, this worldview guides us about the propriety of our behavior.

When this worldview loses its usefulness, a conscious effort is needed to discern the universal principle that governs any given issue, because it is incumbent upon each Muslim to rise above his narrow view of how Islam should be practiced.

91   Roy, *Globalised Islam*, pp. 23–24.

We have seen how the position of the hands in the simple act of standing upright for ritual prayer distinguishes the worshipper's affiliation from that of another. Each school of jurisprudence (Hanafī, Hanbalī, Malikī, Shafi'ī and Ja'farī) enjoins a particular variation on the basic act of prayer.[92] But Muslims also disagree on issues of theological or spiritual import (e.g., Sunnis, Shiites, Sufism, Kharijites, Ahmadiyyah, and others). Add ethnicity to this and you get an idea of the variety of ways of living the Muslim faith. And yet they all call themselves Muslims.

Delinking Islam from local cultures is essential to understanding how the fundaments have informed and shaped its various cultures.

Dynamic sources of Islamic jurisprudence

Local interpretations of Islam are part and parcel of its incredible social and historical continuity. As long as these interpretations remain dynamic, people will continue to put them into practice and realize their human potential. This becomes more difficult when their purpose is to perpetuate old patterns of behavior for their own sake.

"Custom" (*'urf*) can provide a critical source for the creation of an indigenous Islam in Europe. It is valid insofar as it does not contravene the will of God, of which the body of principles Muslims call the Sharī'ah is a legal expression.[93] To

---

92   There are different ways of performing Muslim prayer. The differences are easily observable when one compares a Shiite mosque with a Sunni mosque. Generally, these differences are considered minor. The main principles are observed by all Muslims. All Muslims pray facing Mecca, and the numbers of daily prayers are the same.

93   We often use Sharī'ah (Islamic Law) and *fiqh* (jurisprudence) interchangeably, but they are not the same. If Sharī'ah is the "compass" (God's revelation and the timeless principles derived from them that cannot change), jurisprudence is the "map." This map must conform to the compass, but it reflects specific conditions (time, place, geography, and so on). The compass is fixed; the map is subject to change (Esposito/Mogahed, 2007:53).

be sure, the universality of Islam I am talking about, and from which jurisprudents, scholars, and mystics have long drawn inspiration, is meaningless without the two essential sources of Islam I discussed earlier: the Qur'ān and *Sunnah* (the way of the Prophet Muhammad). However, other sources besides them have informed Islamic jurisprudence, the discipline that defines and governs the duties and rights of the faithful.

Imam Mālik (founder of the Māliki school of jurisprudence) has gone so far as to equate the *'amal ahl al-madinah* (the customary practice of the people of Medina) with *ijmā'* (consensus). Ijmā' has been instrumental in making customs part of the Sharī'ah. It has served as an important vehicle for assimilating customary rules deemed harmonious with the spirit of the Sharī'ah or simply acceptable on the basis of necessity (*darūrah*).

Another source is the recognition of public interest (*maslahah*) and *istihsān* (the value of improvement or reform). Bearing some similarities to natural law, it reflects a "juristic preference" for what is good as opposed to what is less so.

All these elements constitute vital sources of law wherever the Qur'ān and Sunnah alone provide no possibility for an explicit ruling.[94] But I want to focus on two dynamic sources of Islamic jurisprudence that determine common standards for Muslims: *ijtihad* (personal reasoning in the interpretation of Islam) and *'urf* (literally, "that which is known," or custom).

Ijtihad. Muslim scholars in the medieval period contributed handsomely to making ijtihad a vital source of jurisprudence. But ijtihad was never without controversy, and at one time it came to be perceived as invalid when some scholars proclaimed the *doors of ijtihad closed*. But who exactly gave them the authority to do this? God? Prophet Muhammad?

The answer is neither. There is no organized "church" or "priesthood" in Islam.

---

94 Mohammed Hashim Kamali, *Principles of Islamic Jurisprudence*, 3rd ed. (Cambridge: Islamic Texts Society, 2003), p. 372.

And yet many *ulamā*, or Islamic scholars, found it hard to return ijtihād to its rightful role, just when Muslims desperately needed it as an instrument to interpret the divine message under different and constantly changing conditions. Muslims, not only in the West but everywhere, have to avail themselves of what is perhaps the "most important source of Islamic law next to the Qurān and the *Sunnah*."[95] Failing this they will continue to deprive themselves of both a true understanding of the fundamentals of Islam and the orderly means by which to derive legal and moral precepts for life *today*, not yesterday. They need to exercise their power of reason within an authentic, well-rooted frame of reference. The "personal reasoning" practiced within Islam's long tradition of jurisprudential reasoning can, at the very least, provide the beginning of a response to pressing challenges.

'Urf. Custom refers to social practices and should not be mistaken for personal habits or idiosyncrasies. Its recognition within the framework of jurisprudence allows Muslims to more effectively identify and examine the values they share. As Mohammad Hashim Kamali explains, "[T]he *Sharī'ah* has, in principle, accredited approved custom as a valid ground in the determination of its rules relating to *halāl* [lawful] and *harām* [forbidden]."[96] He captures its significance thus:

Customs that were prevalent during the lifetime of the Prophet and were not expressly overruled by him are held to have received his tacit approval and have become part of what is known as *Sunnah taqrīriyyah*. Pre-Islamic Arabian custom which was thus approved by the Prophet was later upheld by the Companions, who often referred to it through statements such as "We used to do such-and-such while the Prophet was alive."

---

95   Ibid., p. 468.
96   Kamali, *Principles of Islamic Jurisprudence*, p. 371.

Islam has thus retained many pre-Islamic Arabian customs while it has at the same time overruled the oppressive and corrupt practices of that society. Islam also attempted to amend and regulate some of the Arab customary laws with a view to bringing them into line with the principles of the *Sharī'ah*. The reverse of this is also true in the sense that pre-Islamic customs of Arabia influenced the *Sharī'ah* in its formative stages of development. Even in the area of the verbal and actual *Sunnah*, there are instances where Arabian custom has been upheld and incorporated within the *Sunnah* of the Prophet. An example of this is the rulings of the *Sunnah* concerning the liability of the kinsmen of an offender (i.e. the *'āqilah*) for the payment of blood money, or *diyah*. Similarly, the *Sunnah* that regulates certain transactions such as mortgage (*rahn*), advance sale (*salam*) and the requirement of equality (*kafā'ah*) in marriage have their roots in pre-Islamic custom of the Arabs. There are also vestiges of pre-Islamic custom in the area of inheritance, such as the significance that the rules of inheritance attach to the male line of relationship, known as the *'asabah*.[97]

Thus, in Islam's formative stage Muslims upheld many pre–Islamic Arabian customary law and customs, overruled those they deemed oppressive and corrupt, and amended others to bring them in line with the principles of the Sharī'ah. In doing so, they effectively incorporated the best of early Arabian custom into the Sunnah of the Prophet. This was only the initial process that started Muslims on the path to a full-fledged civilization. It has not stopped, and indeed cannot stop. The more Muslims progress and the farther they travel the world, the greater the need to revisit universal principles

97 Kamali, *Principles of Islamic Jurisprudence*, p. 372.

before rendering particular judgments that could have long-term repercussions.

So important is the concept of custom to Islam that when Imam al-Shāfi'ī, after laying the foundations of his school of jurisprudence in Iraq, traveled to Egypt, he found that local customs were different from his. His response was to change some of his earlier opinions accordingly, not impose them automatically.[98] If anything, his approach clearly illustrates the role that ijtihād played at that time in harmonizing prevailing custom with the Shari'ah.[99]

Islam is not static.

If customs were so important to a great scholar like al-Shafi'i, then why not systematically explore "Swiss" customs? Islam's recognition of customs places a high premium on healthy social change and dynamic interaction with the social environment. Customs play a vital role in this interaction, just as they in turn are destined to change.

Delinking Islam from culture

The idea of a process of deculturalization of Islam sounds more radical than it really is, so let me clarify.

It requires the adoption of three goals. First, Muslims have to determine the main characteristics of a global Muslim identity (GMI); second, they have to recognize that religious experience and identity must not be stifled by too close a link with any given culture; and third, they must stop seeing Islam as a religion that privileges one custom over another, or

---

98   Ibid., pp. 371–72.
99   One example where a previous ruling was changed has to do with "responsible for damage." Under the rules of *fiqh*, a man who causes harm to another by giving him false information is not responsible for the damage he has caused. The rule of fiqh that applies to this and similar cases is that only the *mubāshir*, the person who acted directly, is responsible for the losses. However, owing to the spread dishonesty and corruption, the later *fuqahā'* have departed from this rule in favor of holding the false reporter responsible for the losses caused (Kamali, *Principles of Islamic Jurisprudence*, p. 381).

disfavors customs altogether (a negative stance typical of the most extreme Islamic revivalists), since Arab and non-Arab Muslims alike have been practicing their respective customs from the very beginning of Islam.

These three aspects are not mutually exclusive, but complementary.

To deny the inclusion of Swiss custom in Muslim practices would be tantamount to dismissing the culture that Swiss Muslims already call their own and, in effect, rejecting a vital source of Islam ('urf). On the contrary, the Muslims of Switzerland (and those of the rest of the West) are duty-bound to question their current practices and delink Islam from its foreign sources of cultures with a view to identifying its universal norms and expected patterns of conduct. From this "transnational" perspective they will be able to contextualize Islam within the compass of Swiss customary practice.

Let me recapitulate what we have considered so far with regard to 'urf.[100]

i. The rules of 'urf are changeable, whereby custom may in the course of time give way to a new custom or disappear altogether with changing circumstances.

ii. 'Urf paves the way for fresh ijtihād, which informs the process by which a ruling may be amended to accommodate a customary practice that has not yet been recognized as 'urf.

iii. The particular customs included in 'urf do not depend on agreement among the *mujtahidūn* (Muslim scholars who are competent to interpret Islamic law) alone, but must be recognized and accepted by the community as a whole.

Acceptance of Swiss 'urf as a valid basis of ijtihād is crucial to putting the Muslim community on the right track. Shying away from it will keep it static and perpetually out of touch. Many rulings of the earliest jurists were changed by their successors based on changes in circumstances and the specific

---

100   Kamali, *Principles of Islamic Jurisprudence*, pp. 375–76.

customs themselves. The Muslims in Switzerland must adopt a similar approach and take the inner dynamics of their country's customs seriously into account. If Imam al-Shāfiʿī was able to do it with respect to Egyptian customs, then Islamic scholars living in the West can, too. ʿUrf is a legitimate part of Islamic law, the key to legal development within new contexts. But it becomes meaningless when we limit it to a single set of customs for all time.

By the same token, it would be incorrect for Swiss Muslims to observe, say, a ruling from Iran that declares a missing (*mafqūq*) person dead. The rules of fiqh (jurisprudence) state that a missing person should be declared dead only at the age at which he or she would normally be expected to die. If jurists in Iran have determined this age to be seventy-one, then the ruling would not be sufficiently relevant for Muslims living in Switzerland or any other country where the life expectancy differs. The Swiss generally live more than eighty years. In Somalia the estimate is around fifty years, and for other countries it is even lower. Therefore, Swiss jurists would have to raise the minimum age for a declaration of death to be valid. Life expectancy varies depending on time and place, and we have not even mentioned gender (women generally live longer than men).

This is what is meant when we say that Muslims cannot practice their religion correctly if they fail to recognize the context.

More reflections on customary practice

Custom may be verbalized (*qawlī*), acted out (*fiʿlī*), or both.

Verbal custom may be as simple as a response to a person sneezing. It is customary to say *al-hamdulillah* when someone sneezes and for the latter to reply *yarhamak Allah*. Both Arabic expressions convey a wish for God's blessing. Would it be un-Islamic for a British Muslim to say "Bless you" or "God bless you" instead? It is a common English expression that expresses the same thing. If the idea is to thank God and to wish God's blessings upon another, what does it matter if one does it in Arabic or English?

One of the unique features of the Qur'ān, the only sacred scripture preserved in its original form, is that it can be read in the language in which it was set down. When they perform *salāt*, therefore, Muslims use the Arabic. But why should it also be compulsory to say, "God bless you" in Arabic?

Muslims who grapple with this question every day perhaps ought to reflect on the Universal Principles of Islam that are supposed to govern their behavior, instead of sticking to a foreign custom that is basically unintelligible in their (new) context, be it British, Canadian, French, or Swiss.

So much for verbal 'urf. Acted-out 'urf consists of practices that have to do with dress, religious celebrations, and so on. Take the example of *thawb*, a men's traditional Arab robe. Ankle length, *thawb* simply means "garment" in Arabic. It may be of any color in the world, but it is usually white; not only that, but it is worn by Arab men of different faiths. Interestingly, thawbs today are worn by many Muslims around the world. Arab by tradition, with no particular religious significance, this style of dress has become standard for devout men everywhere.

Islam has transformed and been profoundly transformed by local African cultures, and as in other regions of the world, Muslims there wear the thawb as part of their "Islamic" dress. The difference is that South Africans call the same garment *jubba*, East Africans *kanzu*, Libyans *suriya*, and Moroccans *gandora*. Besides the kanzu, Kenyans also associate the *hebaya* worn by women with Islam. *Hebaya* is a long, black over-garment robe that is traditional Arab dress and a national dress in Saudi Arabia. Kenyans know it as hebaya but they also have a Swahili name for it, *buibui*. When they leave home, most Swahili women, be they Muslims or non-Muslims, wear a two-piece outfit known as *leso*, where materials are wrapped around like a sari.

Just as some pre-Islamic Arabian customs were retained in the formative stages of Islam, so Islam values local customs elsewhere. Given this, why should the West African *boubou* (a flowing wide-sleeved robe worn by men), the Bangladeshi sari (a strip of colorful unstitched cloth draped over the body and wrapped around the waist worn by some women in South Asia), or the Swahili leso also not be regarded as Islamic? Islamic does not mean Arabized. All these garments and the materials they are made of fulfill the requirements of Islamic law. What matters is that the *awrah* (intimate parts of the body of both men and women) be covered as required by the Sharī'ah. Any discussion on the subject can only revolve around the subject of awrah, not whether thawb or hebaya is the only acceptable dress for Muslims.

Islam is no more monolithic than it is Arab-centric. If the Arabic Qur'an and Arabic ritual prayers have not made it so, then there is no inherent reason for the political structures of Muslims to take the Saudi Arabian monarchy—or, for that matter, the Algerian republic—as the model. And still, many Muslims feel obligated to shed their traditions for Arab ones. This is especially true when it comes to giving names. Muslims generally carry names with Arabic roots, and some converts drop their born names for Arabic ones.

Swiss or Western Muslims in general have a long way to go, but eventually they will comprehend that there is nothing inherently wrong with retaining one's religion *and* culture; the one does not necessarily exclude the other. It is high time they become clear about what Islam is. Africans can be African and remain Muslim at the same time. Europeans can remain European while following Islam. A Swiss woman may call herself Heidi without renouncing her Islam.

It saddens me when non-Arabs mistake Islam for Arab culture, and when some Arabs themselves refuse to see the compatibility of other cultures with Islam. More than thirty years ago, Basam Tibi eloquently portrayed the phenomenon I am talking about:

> During a discussion with Senegalese writers and Arab diplomats in summer 1982 in Dakar, a heated argument arose as to whether drumming could be recognized as an Islamic ritual and whether belief in magic was at all admissible in Islam. For the Senegalese neither of these questions is controversial because drumming and magic both form part of their culture; Arab participants, however, rejected both these phenomena on the grounds that they were "un-Islamic." On another occasion, at an international philosophical conference in November 1979, an Indonesian of religion, Mukti Ali, lectured on the Indonesian conception of Islam; his remarks provoked discord among professors of Al-Azhar University (the oldest Islamic university) because for them there is only one monolithic Islam, based on their own Arabcentric preconception.[101]

Back to basics

The incident described by Tibi reminds me of the time when I recited the Qur'an at the Islamic Center in Lindenrain, Bern. An Algerian complimented me on my *qirāt* (Quran recitation), and then remarked with obvious pride that I had now become an "Arab." I inferred from this sentiment a presumption that I wished to be an Arab in the first, and that one way to be one was to recite the Qur'an well. He was somewhat shocked and surely disappointed when I informed him that I was happy to remain African and that I could be African and still be a "good" Muslim.

101   Bassam Tibi, *Islam and Cultural Accommodation of Social Change*, trans. by Clare Krojzi (San Francisco: Westview Press, 1990), p. 16.

Muslims are commanded to "read" by God, the Most Generous, who *taught man what he knew not by the pen* (Qur'an 96:1–5). This is the first recorded revelation to the man whom God made prophet, Muhammad. It implies learning, not imitation. Indeed, learning is precisely how Arab culture itself has evolved and improved on Arabia's pre-Islamic tradition. However, the culture of learning that subsequently blossomed in Islam reflects the *Muslims'* legendary capacity to face all manner of challenges and conditions. For the most part, they have done it without losing the main thread that binds them as a religious community.

This deep historic attachment to learning empowers them to embrace an independence of thinking already embodied in a long tradition of ijtihad. They can do this thanks to the knowledge and experience they have gained from living in an unprecedented variety of social contexts and historical times.

The task of the modern reformers is to distinguish what is time-specific from what comes directly from the Qur'an and is universally binding.[102] Tibi insists that the "human being has to live according to Koranic commandments, but must at the same time adapt in his ever-changing environment."[103] This is the only way to achieve balance in an ever-changing world. Ignoring it can only diminish identity. I agree with Steven Vertovec and Alisdair Rogers that identity "is a malleable construction that is shaped and reshaped by internal and external influence influences depending on time and context."[104] As radically as Mecca and Medina have changed since the time of the Prophet under the tutelage of the Saudi royal family, the "purity" of Islam paradoxically can be preserved only by embracing change.

John O. Voll, referring to the dynamic nature of a constantly

---

102   Esposito and Mogahed, *Who Speaks for Islam?* p. 53.
103   Tibi, *Islam and Cultural Accommodation of Social Change*, pp. 28–29.
104 Steven Vertovec and Alisdaire Rogers, eds. *Muslim European Youth: Reproducing Ethnicity, Religion, Culture*, (Aldershot: Ashgate, 1998), p. 72.

transforming world, summed it up well: "No society escapes these processes, and old ways of life are disappearing."[105] This, to him, is the challenge that will define the future of Islam. If Voll does not have the authority of an Islamic scholar, then Imam al-Shāfiʿī certainly does, and his view is that changes in time and context affect the practice of Islam.

But let us take the view of a more recent, Egyptian scholar, Rifaʿa al-Tahtawi (1801–73), who spent five years (1826–31) in Paris serving as an imam. He argued that the *ulama'*, or Islamic scholars, are not simply the guardians of a fixed and established tradition. It is incumbent on them to adapt the *Shari'ah* to new circumstances. And if they are properly to interpret the *Shari'ah* in the light of modern needs, they have to understand the nature of the modern world.[106]

The limits

There are limits to which parts of local culture Muslims can celebrate. Those parts have to accord with Islam. Although Muslims are still forbidden to consume a glass of wine at the dinner table, what prevents them from using a knife and fork? Table utensils are not even a European invention, although that is not to say that they are necessarily indigenous to every local Muslim tradition. Nevertheless, in Europe, proper etiquette today demands the use of utensils around the table. How one holds the knife and the fork varies—no big deal.

If the custom does not violate the Sharī'ah, then Muslims are free to incorporate it into their lives. Sometimes it is a question of health or physical comfort. Arabs typically wear thawbs, whereas the Europeans prefer jeans and a pullover. Thawb is a sensible, comfortable article of clothing, especially in hot regions, but why should jeans and a pullover be anathema to Islam? Trousers have been worn by Muslims in cold weather

105   John O. Voll and Osman Bakar, *Asian Islam* (Oxford: Oxford University Press, 2008), p. 285.
106   John L. Esposito and John O. Voll, *Makers of Contemporary Islam* (Oxford: Oxford University Press, 2001), p. 17.

in every historical period. They offer good protection in European's cold climate. Swapping cultures—the Arabization of Switzerland and the Westernization of Saudi Arabia—is totally unnecessary.

- 12 -
Nurturing a Swiss Muslim Tradition: *'Amal Ahl al-Helvetia*

ONTGOMERY WATT TRACED CERTAIN non-Arabian practices that have been Islamized to Judeo-Christian tradition. One example is punishment by stoning, as mentioned in the Qur'an.[107] According to the evidence handed down, "when some Jews asked Muhammad about the punishment of a couple guilty of adultery, he evoked Torah's prescription and ordered the same to be carried out."[108] Another example is

---

107   Montgomery Watt W, "Islam and the Integration of Society," in *The Sociology of Religion*, vol. 2 (London: Rutledge, 1998), pp. 191–92.
108   Ibid. There are several stories on stoning, one of which describes a Jewish rabbi trying to conceal the verse of stoning in his scripture, since it was no longer carried out by the Jewish people. There are also references to a verse on stoning in the Qur'anic revelation, known to the caliph Umar. The normal punishment for adultery at Medina in Muhammad's lifetime was flogging, though initially and in certain cases house detainment was preferred. As more and more Jewish people and Christians became Muslims, they tended to retain the punishment of stoning, with which they were accustomed. Eventually stories began to circulate that stoning had been sanctioned and practiced by Muhammad and some of the leading companions. Although the punishment was officially recognized, it was extremely rare in practice, since "the jurists hedged it in with conditions that could seldom be fulfilled; e.g., four male witnesses must have seen the act" (Ibid., pp. 191–92).

the messianic devotion to the suffering savior (which inspires certain Shiite rituals and beliefs).[109] This is a tradition that dates from the time of Jesus and earlier to the Old Testament. Shi'a ceremonies during the month Muharram express ritual grief for the Prophet's family, particularly of his grandchild Husain ibn Ali, by striking their chests. This tradition of mourning has a long history and "can be traced back to the old myth of Tammuz and beyond."[110]

Now, consider Sufi dance and African celebrations. If we agree that Islam can be "Arab" for Arabs and African for Africans, then Islam can be equally Swiss to the Swiss or generally European to Europeans and even more general, Western to Westerners. No custom has preference in the eyes of God. Several *ayat* (Qur'anic verses) support this, one of which is this one:

خُذِ الْعَفْوَ وَأْمُرْ بِالْعُرْفِ وَأَعْرِضْ عَنِ الْجَاهِلِينَ (7:199)

Keep to forgiveness, enjoin 'urf and turn away from the ignorant

No less a figure than the Mālikī jurist Shihāb al-Dīn al-Qarāfī held that this *āyah* provided clear and explicit authority for *'urf* (custom).[111] Another verse sheds light on the general intention of God for human beings.

وَمَا جَعَلَ عَلَيْكُمْ فِي الدِّينِ مِنْ حَرَجٍ (22:78)

This āyah teaches, additionally, that *God has not laid upon you any hardship in religion.* This is clear when we consider that a wholesale rejection of Arabian customs would have caused immense hardship to the people, and the Prophet's rulings have since formed part of his *Sunnah* (words and practices of Prophet Muhammad). One example of rulings considered

---

109   Watt, "Islam and the Integration of Society", pp. 191–92.
110   Ibid.
111   Kamali, *Principles of Islamic Jurisprudence*, p. 379.

consistent with the Sunnah has to do with the liability of the kinsmen of an offender (i.e., the *'āqilah*) and the payment of "blood money." Its acceptance depended on whether or not it conflicted with the *nusūs* (clear general principles and objectives) of the Sharī'ah.

Muslims needed a good amount of critical thinking in their search for the universal principles of Islam underlying the five categories into which they had divided behavior and practices: *wājib* (dutiful), *mandūb* (preferable), *harām* (forbidden), *makrūh* (abominable), and *mubāh* (permissible). What the Swiss Muslims require today is an equally well-reasoned and well-rooted foundation upon which to develop what I call *'amal ahl al-Helvetia* (the customary practice of the people of Switzerland). This alone will free them from the cultural limitations hindering their progress.

From Universal Islam to Western Muslim

Once they identify the fundamental, universal principles of Islam, Muslims will be in a far better position to challenge any worldview holding sway in their community that has outlived its usefulness. At this stage, the object is to return to the concrete reality in which Muslims live. Equipped with a deeper understanding of Universal Islam, they can approach customary Swiss practices with more honesty and enterprise.

Although this process has to take place within the fold of Islam's collective experience, the universality of Islam embraces all human beings without expunging their differences. This approach leads to a questioning of the old ways and views accumulated over time. The early Muslims had to do it when the Prophet challenged them to act as an *ummah* (community of Islam) rather than as a people bound together by nothing more than tribal allegiances. If it can happen again in our times, just as it has with every generation, then dialogue should not be the insurmountable challenge that right-wing politicians—not to mention some insular Muslims—have made it out to be.

A new cultural synthesis has to take place among the Muslims of Switzerland that is firmly rooted in their highest principles, because the implications of failure should give pause. Having embraced the best of Swiss culture into their lives, Muslims would be in a far better position to enter into dialogue with fellow Swiss. There, the citizens of different faiths and ideologies may meet and talk and interact.

Moreover, they would no longer need to do so only within the framework of a high-profile "dialogue among civilizations," as laudable as this idea is for *nations* to pursue, but as full participants within the distinct borders of each nation-state. Before such a meeting of minds can bear fruit, each party first has to come to terms with its own identity and past. The fear of foreigners is no longer an excuse; it is self-serving to see oneself as the pinnacle of perfection. But are politicians mature enough to cast away their stereotypes of one side or the other? Are Muslims mature enough to call Swiss society their own?

Both they and all concerned non-Muslims have to think critically about these matters. There is no other way for Swiss Muslims and non-Muslims to cultivate a dynamic, healthy, and forward-looking culture. Without questioning their own worldviews they will be hard-pressed to envisage culture, education, beliefs, political views, and life experiences shaping their common future.

Pursuit of social stability

By now you should know that accommodating Western social customs constitutes an internally negotiated process, and that it can realistically be done thanks to Islam's long and complex legal tradition. This tradition is a product of the care with which Islamic jurisprudence has sought to transcend ethnic and even sectarian boundaries to meet the demands of the faith. It can meet the demands of secular governance, if by *secular* we mean the interdiction of favoritism, nepotism, and discrimination of any kind. For centuries these ills have beset practically every society. There cannot be "us" and "them" inside national boundaries.

I am reminded of a true story related by Edward W. Said of about eighty Arab and Jewish youth musicians grouped together by a talented musician, Barenboim, to play in an orchestra.[112] They practiced daily for hours, and then at night they discussed culture, art, and politics. Egyptians, Israelis, Lebanese, and Palestinians came together out of a single desire to play music. They all admired Beethoven and Mozart, and all wanted to play in an orchestra. Each musician contributed in his or her way to the *collective* success of the orchestra.

If this group of Arabs and Jewish people could find unity through love of music, despite the political fires raging around them, then Muslims and non-Muslims in Switzerland too can work with single-minded purpose in the pursuit of social stability. Whatever conflicts exist between them can be dealt with and transformed. Indeed, every crisis can be an opportunity. On the one side are the Western host societies: they have to *want* to understand, not simply recoil at the Muslim stereotypes foisted upon the public. On the other side lie the Muslims: they have to reflect upon the worldviews either bequeathed to them by the lands of origin or developed right here under the severe pressure of discrimination. Once they understand—not just acknowledge—the universality of Islam, they will find the unity they need to find common cause with any group ready to accommodate them.

What if the flutist or percussionist in the young orchestra insisted that his participation be recognized as the best—i.e., the "model" to which everyone else ought to look up? What kind of music would have resulted? What if, on top of that, any of the musicians had failed to master his or her instrument? As it happened, each musician contributed something positive, which the orchestra incorporated. At the same time each also

112   Al-Maaly, *Die Arabische Welt*, p. 81.

had to demonstrate an unflagging commitment to improving his or her skill through practice.

The present crisis will lose its bite and peaceful coexistence will take root when both parties share the common goal of bettering the whole through self-understanding. Nothing will be achieved if one party forces the other to bend to the will—right or wrong.

How much would society as a whole benefit from such a relationship? I am hopeful that the present difficulties will be turned into an opportunity for progress.

Acculturation is a long process

The cultural synthesis I seek for Swiss Muslims revolves around a broad internal dynamic that incorporates self-identity, self-criticism, cultural selection, and the search for internal coherence. Amado M. Padilla defines acculturation as "a complex interactional process involving both members of the cultural group undergoing change and members of the host culture."[113] A new process is needed to transform both the Muslim and the local communities into a new, shared culture of dynamic interaction.

If I am correct in holding that cultures and religions are never static, then even the obstacles to interaction cannot withstand the tide of cultural change. Nevertheless social identities do not simply melt away at the first sign of crisis; in fact, the evidence points to their hardening. How well they endure depends on the unifying force of their shared values. Any changes they undergo, as Lawrence Rosen explains, have to take place on the basis of "give-and-take." But change remains inevitable, as

---

113   Amado M. Padilla, "The role of Cultural Awareness and Ethnic Loyalty in Acculturation," in *Acculturation: Theory, Models and Some New Findings* (Boulder: Westview Press, 1980), p. 48.

no culture can help being affected by another, no matter how strong it is.[114]

When Muslims refer to themselves as an ummah, they mean it in the sense of *ummah Islamiyyah* (Islamic community). Like every conceivable community, it exhibits diversity, which Islam sanctions. Therefore, nothing in Islam prevents Muslims from extending the concept of ummah to the community of citizens residing in Switzerland: *ummah Swisriyyah* (Swiss community). Many people, one nation. It has a secular ring that complements, rather than contradicts, the terminology to which Muslims are accustomed, and it corresponds to a modern vision of Switzerland.

For this to happen, Islam must be fully recognized as part of the Western world, just as Muslims must see themselves wholly as Swiss, Europeans, or Westerners. It would signal the rise of a unique Swiss custom.

It is not a big stretch for Muslims. Historically, they evolved from their ethnic crucible in the Prophet's lifetime to a full-fledged civilization, and now millions of them live in the politico-cultural sphere of Europe and North America. There, the dynamics of interaction and cultural exchange, not the lethargy of a superficial stability, will determine how well they fare in the struggle to improve society for everyone. Ideally, they will also move away from the line of crossfire, where they have been pushed by circumstance.

---

114   Lawrence Rosen, *The Culture of Islam: Changing Aspects of Contemporary Muslim Life* (Chicago: University of Chicago Press, 2004), p. 145.

PART V
Tribulations of the Swiss

- 13 -
The Reformist Voices of Muslims

IN VIEW OF THE millions of Muslims who hold European passports, Frank J. Bulis and Jan Rath remind us that "the Muslim communities have developed in such a way—in most countries they encompass a number of generations—that the use of the term 'immigrant' becomes increasingly debatable."[115]

The stigmatization of immigrants—the word has indeed come to suggest social stigma—is symptomatic of the kind of intercommunity interaction that many like me think should be eased off the stage. Clearly, Muslims have their part to play in creating the right conditions for this to change. Islam is a universal religion, and it did not come into existence yesterday. It is not even new to Europe, no matter how much some may deny this heritage. Muslims have been in contact with peoples in Europe for so long that it should not be an insurmountable challenge to find a workable remedy for the present tensions.

Many Muslim thinkers have grappled with this possibility. I would like to review how some of them have talked about the major questions Muslims face in the West. Several notable works

---

115   Frank J. Bujis and Jan Rath, *Muslims in Europe: The State of Research* (Essay prepared for the Russell Sage Foundation, New York, 2003).

have outlined ways for going forward, the most promising of which, in my opinion, suggest a European-Muslim identity: *being* European Muslims and *practicing* a Euro-Islam.

Those who advocate this position have attempted essentially to mediate between Islam and the specific conditions of modernity under which Muslims in the West exist. To them Islam is compatible with modern democracy and tolerance. They can think in these terms because they have taken the trouble to reread Islam and its authentic sources in the light of changing circumstances. They seek to expand Islam's reach by extending its longstanding capacity to reason out problems and by using modern approaches derived mainly from the social sciences.

The result so far has been a healthy revision that, in part, proposes the abolition or abrogation of certain Islamic laws that have grown irrelevant to Muslims' current needs and aspirations.[116] To the reformists, essentially, if it is not *harām* to be both Muslim and Arab at the same time, then it should be halāl to be Muslim and European, Muslim and American, and so forth.

Reformists take the initiative

Two distinct currents have emerged over the last century and a half: one reformist, the other conservative. The main difference between them is in how Islam should be read. The reformist intellectuals are reformist by virtue of their liberalized, rationalist, and contextualized approach to the interpretation of Islamic scriptural and legal sources. They seek interpretations of Islamic sources that are relevant to Muslims' current conditions and not simply conformist. To them, reconciling reason with faith is not just an intellectual exercise. They value pluralism and tolerance, not to mention constructive interaction and dialogue with other cultures.

---

116   Shireen T. Hunter, ed. *Reformist Voices of Islam: Mediating Islam and Modernity* (New York: M. E. Sharpe, 2009), p. 3.

And their views are antithetical to the theory of the clash of civilizations, which predicts a clash between Islam and the West.

The opposite discourse is "conservative," at least insofar as its proponents seek a literalist understanding of Islamic sources. Historically, literalism in the technical sense and as a school of thought was once marginal to the mainstream, even extreme, but it has gained so much currency in our times that it practically passes for "tradition." Basically, literalism requires total devotion to a vision of the past based on a utopian interpretation of the life of the Prophet and his companions, who serve as the sole literal model for all legal rulings and gender relations.

Some offshoots of this current have taken to violence, since the larger society has largely proved resistant to their views. In response, they go so far as to declare fellow Muslims "infidels." I would say that this latter coterie of violent militants probably constitutes the best "evidence" that the theory for a clash of civilizations can come up with.

Although both reformists and literalists share in their claim to restore the original purity of Islam, "reformists emphasize the restoration of Islam's spiritual rather than ritualistic dimension, the recapturing of true spirit, which they believe has been buried under layers of ritual and legal constructs, and the achievement of its ultimate, and so far forgotten and unaccomplished mission, which is to establish justice, mercy, and respect for human dignity."[117]

To anyone unfamiliar with Islam's intellectual history, this debate may appear novel. As Hunter put it, though, "the issue of reform and renewal and the debate about what constitutes reform are nothing new, and date to Islam's early history."[118] Sayyid Jamal al-Din Afghani (1838–97) and Sheikh Muhammad Abduh (1849–1905) are rightly recognized as the

117 Hunter, *Reformist Voices of Islam*, p. 4.
118 Ibid.

originators of this new conception of Islam. Since then, many differences have surfaced among Muslim reformers, but their principal motivations and ultimate goals remained. They may be summarized as follows:

1. Return to the basic sources of Islam, namely the Qur'an and the Sunnah.

2. Restoration of Muslims' faith and morality.

3. Intellectual, economic, and political revitalization of the Muslim world.

4. Strengthening the Islamic community and defending it against internal and external enemies.

5. Ensuring Islam's continued relevance to Muslims' lives in all its dimension.[119]

The major issues that have erupted in Western Europe have to do with veiling, gender relations, honor killing, animal slaughtering, exclusive cemeteries, and political participation versus violence. Although not new, these issues are being debated and written about ad nauseam. But the reformists have not shrunk from their duty to sort out the issues.

Perhaps the most prominent scholar among them today trying to make a difference for Muslims living in the Islamic and Western worlds is Sheikh Yusuf al-Qardawi. He has been called a *transnational 'alim*—a "global mufti," according to the title of a recent book.[120] In 2008, *Foreign Policy Magazine* placed him third on its list of the top twenty intellectuals worldwide, describing the European Fatwa Council he heads as one of the "most important transnational organizations." The council focuses on adapting Islamic jurisprudence to the needs of Europe's Muslim population.

119   Ibid.
120   Bettina Gräf and Jakob Skovgaard, *Global Mufti: the Phenomenon of Yusūf al-Qaradāwi* (New York: Colombia University Press, 2009).

Another prominent, "global" Muslim intellectual is a Swiss-born Egyptian called Tariq Ramadan. His new message to European Muslims is intended to "transcend culturally particularistic tendencies."[121] He has written extensively on all manner of topics; his books include *Islam, the West and the Challenges of Modernity, To Be a European Muslim,* and most recently, *Radical Reform: Islamic Ethics and Liberation* and *The Quest for Meaning: Developing a Philosophy of Pluralism.*

All these works call for reform and encourage European Muslims to find commonalities with the traditions that have evolved in Europe. He urges them to adapt what is best in them to the loftiest norms in Islam. Aside from the *'ibadat* (ritual obligations), he sees wide room for adaptation in the *muamalat* (social relations). In general his studies demonstrate that leading a devoted Islamic life is possible in a pluralistic society. Similarly to what I have argued in the case of *'urf* (custom), Ramadan argues, for instance, that Islam simply requires Muslims to dress modestly. How different societies choose to dress is subject to any number of factors; hence, their only obligation is to dress or to carry out other practices according to their best understanding. Above all, he advises the Muslims of Europe to be *European Muslims.* Indeed, practicing Islam in a European context and actively participating in the social, political, and economic life are essential to ensuring their Islam remains alive and healthy.

Another Muslim scholar, Bassam Tibi—a Syrian with German citizenship—advocates for the reform of Islam and has coined the concept of "Euro-Islam." He argues that a "clash of civilizations" can be avoided, on the one hand, if Muslims accept the secular model and practice their religion without Shari'ah and jihad; and on the other, if Westerners looked beyond narrow ethnicity as a standard for citizenship. This is how Muslims will be able to reach full integration and be

121   Hunter, *Reformist Voices of Islam,* p. 253.

"citizens of the heart." Tibi derived his concept of "Euro-Islam" from personal observations while in West Africa, where he discovered an "Africanized Islam." If the Senegalese could adapt their faith within their indigenous environment, he concluded, then Muslims in Europe could do the same within theirs. The only difference is that the customs of the Senegalese are those of Senegal. Immigrants and their children, on the other hand, have to adopt the customs of a new home. The "Europeanization" of Islam is possible. According to Tibi, however, the reform of Islam in Europe implies important cultural changes. Only through change will a vibrant Euro-Islam finally take shape.

Tibi has argued that the idea of a clash of civilizations has arisen only because of differing *Weltanschauungen* (worldviews)— one Weltanschauung European, the other Islamic. But if the secular model of European identity is inclusive enough, and if Muslims follow an open Islam that is not attached to either Shari'ah or jihad, then there is no sense of continuing to speak of a clash.[122] The best chance for peaceful coexistence among immigrants, their descendants, and native Europeans is to have common values, or *Werteorintierungen*, which in the end would be both European and Euro-Islamic in character.

According to Tibi, the common denominators with respect to values are as follows[123]:

- Separation of religion and politics
- Secular democracy
- Individual (not collective) human rights
- Secular tolerance in the sense of respect for others and for believers of other faiths
- Civil society and institutions
- Pluralism that combines rules with the cultural diversity of Werteorintierung

---

122   Bassam Tibi, *Euro-Islam: Die Lösung eines Zivilisationskonflikts* (Darmstadt: Primus Verlag, 2009), p. 10.
123   Tibi, *Euro-Islam*, pp. 43–44.

Many other reform-minded Muslims have dedicated their works to the Westernization of Islam or have debated and written about Islam and modernity. They share a deep attachment to Islam's beginnings and subsequent flowering. Sociologist Nadia Fadil perceives a consensus forming among them that only the adaptation of Islam to its Western social environment would enable Muslims to be full citizens.[124] This vision is still some ways away from realization, and reform has not always been seen positively by others, who label it *bid'a* (harmful innovation) and thus "heretical."[125]

Europe is temporarily embroiled in an "Islam versus West" debate that seems to prevent us from picturing the future in the form of a "Europeanized Islam" and in a sense, conversely, "Islamized Europe." The more right-wing politicians busy themselves with the politics of hate, the less Muslims are seen as participating enough in the social life of the country. Not that the idea of their participation will ever endear itself to this brand of politicians.

---

124   Nadia Fadil, "Muslim Girls in Belgium: Individual Freedom Through Religion?" Online in *ISIM Newsletter*, no. 13 (2003): p. 18.
125   Hunter, *Reformist Voices of Islam*, p. 4.

- 14 -
What Is Wrong with Switzerland?

FOR TOO LONG, MUSLIMS have suffered the consequences of having a small group in their midst bent on distorting Islam and removing its historic tolerance for diversity. In Switzerland, their best cheerleaders are an outside group: right-wing politicians who have no qualms about playing the racism card. Together they present a serious challenge to reform.

One major challenge pertains to the Federal Constitution of the Swiss Confederation. Under the Federal Constitution, in Article 15, Switzerland must provide for freedom of religion and conscience:

i. Freedom of religion and conscience is guaranteed.
ii. Everyone has the right to choose freely their religion or their philosophical convictions, and to profess them alone or in community with others.
iii. Everyone has the right to join or to belong to a religious community, and to follow religious teachings.
iv. No one shall be forced to join or belong to a religious community, to participate in a religious act, or to follow religious teachings.

These four "principles" of Article 15 leave no doubt about

what the law guarantees. One cannot help asking how exactly the total ban on minaret construction respects "guaranteed" rights in Switzerland.

But we have to recall that the Swiss Federal Constitution also guarantees citizens the right to launch a federation-wide popular initiative for amendments to the Constitution (Article 139), if the signatures of 100,000 citizens can be gathered within eighteen months. This sounds very democratic, but the possibility of amending and creating new laws can have wide repercussions. It can effectively remove the guarantee upon any right, in this case the freedom of religion.

The result is that rights in Switzerland have been rendered theoretical, at best. Minorities such as Muslims and Jewish people are suddenly no longer guaranteed their freedoms. This is the paradox of Swiss direct democracy, despite some safeguards against the aberrant results of referenda. The authorities still have to voice an opinion on a popular proposal.

In the case of the anti-minaret initiative, the Swiss Federal Council (*der Bundesrat*) and the parliament recommended rejection. Below is an excerpt from the Federal Administration's press release at the time.[126]

The popular initiative against the construction of minarets has been submitted in accordance with the applicable regulations, but infringes guaranteed international human rights and contradicts the core values of the Swiss Federal Constitution. Such a ban would endanger peace between religions and would not help to prevent the spread of fundamentalist Islamic beliefs. In its Opinion, passed on Wednesday, the Federal Council therefore recommends that the

126 "Council Opposes Building Ban on Minarets: Opinion on the Popular Initiative Against the Construction of Minarets" (in 27-08-2008 at ejpd.admin.ch).

Swiss parliament reject the initiative without making a counter-proposal.

Clearly, the Swiss Federal Council believed the anti-minaret initiative to be irreconcilable with the human rights guaranteed by the European Convention on Human Rights (ECHR) and the UN Covenant on Civil and Political Rights (UN Covenant II). They gave four reasons why banning minarets on Swiss soil is inconsistent with the basic principles of the constitution.

i. Violates religious freedom and the discrimination ban: In particular, the initiative violates the principle of freedom of religion. Although the ECHR and the UN Covenant II permit religious freedoms to be restricted under certain conditions, those conditions are not fulfilled here. A general ban on the construction of minarets in Switzerland cannot be justified by the protection of public safety and order. It would rule out the necessary review of reasonableness on a case-by-case basis. Furthermore, the initiative disregards Switzerland's ban on discrimination. It targets an Islamic religious symbol in isolation while leaving the comparable symbolic constructions of other religions untouched.

ii. Contradicts the core values of the Federal Constitution: In addition, this initiative, which purports to protect social and legal order in Switzerland, contradicts a number of the basic rights and principles that are rooted in the Federal Constitution: the principle of equality before the law and the ban on discrimination, the freedoms of religion and conscience, the constitutional guarantee of the right of ownership, the principle of proportionality and the observance of international law. A ban on the construction of minarets would also represent a disproportionate degree of interference in cantonal power. Based on their applicable building and spatial planning laws, local authorities are best placed to determine whether or not a construction project should go ahead. There is no reason to deviate from this tried-and-tested system with regard to buildings for a specific religious community.

iii. Ineffective in the fight against extremism: If the aim of the initiative is to put a stop to the growing influence of Islam in Switzerland, it will not achieve this with a general building ban on minarets. Neither does the proposal represent an appropriate means of preventing and combating violence on the part of extremist fundamentalist groups. Federal and cantonal regulations on both domestic security and non-Swiss individuals already provide for effective measures to prevent such activities and protect Switzerland's constitutional foundations. The provisions governing the activities of foreign imams in Switzerland are an example here.

iv. Endangers peace between religions; hinders integration: A ban on minaret construction might endanger peace between religions and hinder the integration of the Muslim population—the overwhelming majority of whom respect Switzerland's legal and social order. Finally, the passing of this popular initiative would not only be met by consternation among the international community, but would also damage Switzerland's standing around the world. This might, in turn, have a negative impact on the security of Swiss facilities and the interests of the Swiss economy. Like members of other religious communities, Muslims in Switzerland cannot invoke their faith to justify non-observance of universally applicable laws. As such, the state has no cause to impose stricter rules on the practice of this faith.

In spite of the fact that a ban on minarets would *violate religious freedom* and *contradict the core values of the Federal Constitution*, the Swiss Federal Constitution, Article 72(3), today reads, "The construction of minarets is prohibited."

How to respond?

Nine years before this law came into force, Farhan Afshar—a Swiss sociologist of Iranian origin and president of the Coordination of Islamic Organizations in Switzerland—wrote about Islam in Switzerland.[127] He pointed out that there was a fundamental contradiction between the constitutional protection of freedom of religion and the constitutional condition whereby no guarantee of religious freedom can exist without the support of the majority. Since Muslims represent a minority, their religious freedom depends entirely on the largesse of the majority. They may be denied protection to practice their religion, and of course the right even to decorate their garagelike mosques with minarets.

Some opponents of the initiative declared the ruling null and void, arguing that it contradicted basic principles enshrined in the Swiss Federal Constitution and the European Convention on Human Rights. The proponents, on the other hand, demanded that the referendum be implemented and threatened to seek a new referendum if the results were annulled.

But what would a nullification of the vote or introduction of another initiative for a ban have done? It probably would not have further induced Muslims to tackle the issues facing their community. Muslims are prevented from enjoying the full rights of Swiss and European citizens.

A history of discrimination

To understand the significance of what happened and, perhaps, to begin the healing process, one has to go back and examine Swiss history.

Switzerland has a reputation for being resistant to social change and to the open-mindedness that can lead to such change. Swiss women—all mothers, sisters, and daughters—were last in Europe before Liechtenstein to be granted suffrage. Only in 1971 were they accorded voting rights at the federal

---

127   De Mortages, *Muslime und schweizerische Rechtsordnung,* pp. 189–95.

level. To this day Swiss women lag behind their counterparts in other Western countries—politically, socially, and economically. And they are significantly behind men, earning less even with the same qualifications for the same work. Voters finally agreed that working mothers should be legally entitled to paid maternity leave only in 2004, a provision that didn't come fully into force until July 2005.

No doubt, women's position has progressively improved over time, and perhaps Switzerland simply needs time to open-up itself on the matter of gender equality to meet modern standards. However, consider the historical precedents of anti-Islam. Muslims have to look at the whole picture before giving up too quickly.

In August 1893, the *Schächtverbot* (Prohibition of Ritual Slaughtering) was voted in exclusively, of course, by men (or *Männervolks*). Josef Lang had this to say about the vote in his article "Gestern die Juden, heute die Muslime" ("Yesterday the Jews, today the Muslims").[128] "Ostensibly it was about animal protection, in reality it was about anti-Semitism. The main theme was the threat of the 'Christian Switzerland' from the 'Eastern Jews,' these strangers from the East" [*my translation*].

If anti-Jewish voices once hid behind animal protection in the prohibition on ritual slaughter, anti-Muslim voices today use security to prohibit the decoration of mosques with minarets (which they liken to missiles). Where *Judaisierung* (Judaization) had once threatened "Christian Switzerland," it is now *Islamisierung* (Islamization) that looms. *Jude-phobia* has mutated into Islamophobia. As the saying goes, "*Egal wer der Feind ist—Hauptsache, es gibt einen* ("No matter who the enemy is, the main thing is that there is one").

Consider also the obstacles that the Swiss citizen of one canton encounters in another canton. In some cases, as far

---

128   Andrea Gross, et al. *Von der Provokation zum Irrtum: Menschenrechte und Demokratie nach dem Minarett-Bauverbott* (St-Ursanne: Editions le Doubs, 2010), p. 78.

as his hosts are concerned, he is a foreigner. If only Muslims opened their ears to what the residents of Zürich, Bern, and Basel say about one another. It is not a secret; many Swiss admit to this behavior. While at a seminar at the University of Basel in 2010, during the "get-to-know-each-other" exercise, I was surprised to hear two Swiss students admit how difficult their integration had been since moving to another canton.

The Swiss too need to think long and hard about their society and the attitudes they take for granted. Before pegging fault to foreignness, and essentially Islamizing problems such as domestic violence, they should contemplate how *both* parties to a conflict could contribute to the resolution. Constructive dialogue begins with such an idea. The refusal to uphold Muslims' complete rights amounts to a denial of Switzerland as their home. It is a hard pill to swallow, but this is precisely what Muslims were asked to accept when the minaret-ban initiative became law.

As Farhan Afshar points out, if Muslims do not feel accepted in Swiss society, how could they continue to participate in or be integrated into it? Why should they give their maximum for a better Switzerland?[129] A failure of integration hinders rather than advances society.

Switzerland's political leaders, hardliners included, should stop and reflect. What are the hindrances to integration?

Afshar argues that the main issues affecting the Muslim community in Switzerland are soluble through mediation. Consider some of these issues:[130]

1. Style of dress, in particular headscarf and veil.

2. The right to abstain from taking part in mixed swimming lessons at school.

---

129 Pahud De Mortages and Tanner, *Muslime und schweizerische Rechtsordnung*, pp. 189–95.
130 Ibid.

3. Allowing Islamic ritual burial.

4. Loosening of the law to legalize ritual slaughtering.

5. Public legal recognition of Islam as an officially recognized religion.

However, the trouble with mediation at this stage is that Muslims lack representation. A body of representatives can lead them into constructive dialogue, but they have no leadership in the true sense.

Is this a reason not to enter dialogue?

No. There is no time to waste. But Muslims have to train their religious clerics for work in Switzerland and to make a community-wide effort to find promising leaders for the coming period.

Switzerland has made great strides since the Middle Ages, but this is not enough. Perhaps its people need more time. Its mothers, sisters, and daughters waited a long time before obtaining equal political rights. Imagine the road ahead for Muslims.

The status quo is unsustainable, and yet Muslims have no choice but to ride out the latest wave of intolerance. Perhaps we all need patience if we are to do this right.

- 15 -
Switzerland's Dilemma

THE LAST CHAPTER ENDED with a note on the training of Islamic clerics, a subject I have mentioned intermittently so far in this book. My insistence on the importance of having clerics trained in the Western context pertains to the need for both a deeper self-understanding and the ability to engage non-Muslims. Reform-minded thinkers and scholars of Islam can help the community achieve both, and Muslims living in the West should familiarize themselves with their ideas. However, they urgently need their imams, not just their intellectuals, to be part of one of the Western world's most venerable institutions: higher education.

The paradox is that although Muslims count many good intellectuals in their ranks, the latter have no grounding in Islam's religious sciences. By the same token, few imams hold Western university diplomas.

The result is a disconnect between two very important spheres of intellectual activity in Islam. So far the debate on "European Islam" has been confined largely to one of these two spheres: among the intellectuals. A Western-educated clergy equipped to carry out the debate inside the mosques, at the grassroots level, would be a game changer.

Identifying the real issues

I do not mean to diminish the value of independent study. This route has been important to many thinking Muslims, given how much individuals have had to rely on their own resources to tackle the burning issues of the day. To be sure, modern communication and technology have made this task far easier. Instead of waiting for guidance from their imams, many Muslims have seized a historic opportunity to inform themselves and to formulate their own questions and opinions. Taking stock of their community, they have consciously striven to separate the fundamental principles of Islam from rigid custom passed down to them.

In the West the main hindrances to this healthy process are played out largely within the family. Therefore, it is first within the "family," the first school in customs, where one must look for long-lasting solutions.

Nina Clara Tiesler quotes Tariq Ramadan, who poignantly summarizes the dilemmas that confront Muslim families across Europe.

One could present Islam, and this often happens inside European Muslim families, by means of a whole series of rules, interdictions or prohibitions, rulings which explain Islam within the framework of a specific relation of protection from an environment which is perceived as too permissive and even hostile. This was, mainly, the attitude of the first generation whose members, with a weak knowledge of Islam, sought first to protect themselves from the loss of their traditions. This latter concept represented, in fact, a vague idea, an indistinct mix of different kinds of elements such as familial or local tradition imported from the country of origin, with its own peculiar rules and principle (and sometimes superstitions), without necessarily being

137

linked to Islam, but often confused with it, or to a clear idea of what is the content of their identity.[131]

Although the reigning fear is the loss of faith, in reality it has more to do with losing the *traditions* to which they feel duty-bound. This is the real dilemma that first-generation European Muslims and, to a diminishing extent, their children, face.

If there is one social institution among Muslims that is ridden with customs, distorted beliefs, and false assumptions, it is marriage. In the course of my research I had the opportunity to make firsthand observations of an interesting mind-set among six Somali interviewees. They all carried Swiss nationality cards. Three of them went to school and completed their apprenticeship in Switzerland, and later went on to take Somali wives who lived in Saudi Arabia and Yemen. (Somalis are connected with other Somalis around the world through family and clan kinships.)

The story is not much different with Muslims of other ethnicities. A youth worker once shared stories with me about the ways in which Muslim Albanian youths thought about sex and marriage. Youths (between fifteen and twenty years old) of Balkan background told him that they have girlfriends more for fun, adding that when they were ready for marriage, they would take "real" women from their ancestral homeland. Although premarital sex is not "customary," strictly speaking, it gives us a glimpse into how custom intervenes in the lives of young people to create a gulf between faith and practice.

Aziz Al-Azmeh, affiliated with a British-Pakistani marriage bureau, found there was "a growing tendency for men in Britain to seek wives from Pakistan rather than from British-bred Pakistani women, and of the former they are choosing

131   Nina Clara Tisler. "Muslime in Europa: Religion und Identitätspolitiken unter veränderten gesellschaftlichen Verhältnissen," in *Politik & Kultur*, Band 8. (Berlin: LIT Verlag, 2006), p. 88.

increasingly younger and more cloistered girls of more conservative outlook."[132]

Interestingly, the social worker told me that the Albanian female teenagers he knew harbored hopes that ran opposite to those of their male cohorts. They wanted neither to import nor to take husbands of the same ethnic origin as themselves. Their preference was for men of different ethnicities, including Swiss.

Yet, all the Muslims I interviewed agreed that establishing an *Imam Ausbildung*, or training course for imams in Switzerland, might offer them an opportunity to understand their situation and to facilitate their integration into the wider society. Sadly, of all those I interviewed, only one Muslim (with a doctoral degree) was informed about the discourse initiated by the religious reformists. The rest sought comfort in a black-or-white view where they had to be committed either to their faith or to a Western life.

I say "sadly" because reform-minded Muslim religious intellectuals offer what I call the "radical middle way" that merges Islamic and European identities. There, not everything Swiss is automatically desirable or need be adopted. This is the dynamic essence of what I call Helvetia Muslims. It is concrete, not universally applicable to any other part of the world. Each country has its own context; thus, the concept of Euro-Islam applies only to the politico-cultural sphere of Europe. Unlike the universalizing vision of Westernization of the world, now anachronistic, Euro-Islam is neither *the* Islam nor universalism.[133]

Modernization versus Westernization

As concretely adapted to its unique context as Islam has to be, the key to reform on a European scale lies in the ability to

132   Aziz Al-Azmeh, *Islam and Modernities*, 3rd ed. (London: Verso, 2009), p. 3.
133   Bassam Tibi (22/03/2007), "Europeanisation, Not Islamisation," Online in *signandsight.com* [accessed October 24, 2010].

distinguish between what is modern and what is Western. There is no doubt that the world has undergone "Westernization." This is not qualitatively different from the Arabization of the earliest converts to Islam, or other instances where one people absorbed another.

Westernization is most starkly observable in dress. The formal dress code for men almost everywhere in the world is the suit, which has become so universal, it may safely be regarded as simply modern. Nothing writ in heaven commands men to wear a suit, but even if the notion of *modern* cannot be separated from that of *Western,* then wearing anything else may be considered improper or even disrespectful. Imagine a German Swiss turning up dressed in an *agwada* or a sari in parliament. It would be so out of context that one could not help asking why that person insisted on dressing that way.

Though conceivable as a scenario, technically no morality is involved in how a person chooses to dress. What one specifically wears rests entirely on personal choice. Muslims are under no religious obligation to dress in anything, as long as it is decent and proper.

Muslims should not mistake Westernization for modernization. They need only look at the case of Africa to see exactly how this has led to a dead end. Sub-Saharan Africans have distanced themselves from indigenous traditions and cultures, yet have retained the worst aspects of tribalism. This state of affairs has had widespread repercussions for their economic development. So much so that the "abject failure of almost all development techniques adopted so far ... is forcing African policy-makers to rethink and review the relevance of tradition for development and growth."[134] There is good reason for a thorough rethinking. Cultural Westernization

---

134   Ali A. Mazrui, *Africanity Redefined*, ed. by Ricardo Rene Laremont and Tracia Leacock Seghatolislami (Asmara, Eritrea: Africa World Press, 2002), p. 71.

is jeopardizing Africa rather than leading it to economic modernization, though even here Africans are "westernizing in the wrong areas of Western culture. Africa westernized in prayer, but not in production; in idiom but not in innovation; in costume but not in computers."[135]

In addition to their new Western dress code African Christians have adopted European names. Like those Muslims who mistake Islam for Arabic culture by taking Arab names, such as Ali and Aisha, African Christians too have opted for European names to exhibit their Christian faith. Even when they inherit tribal names, they will receive one more name— Michael, Margret or some other.

Acculturation may be a worldwide phenomenon, but it is high time to separate Westernization (i.e., Europeanization) from modernization.

By the same token, those Muslims who seek to Arabize themselves do so without enough reflection, because the elements of Arab culture they adopt for their new social environment, whether they are Arabs or not, will not likely profit them. European Muslims should take a page from the Koreans and the Japanese. These two peoples prospered economically and are today ranked among the most industrious in the world. How did they do it? By adopting "mainly the more productive elements of Western civilization" and linking those "to their own methods of social organization and cultural modification."[136] A short while ago their gross domestic product was in the same per-capita category as that of Ghana and Kenya today. True, Ghanaians and Kenyans speak much better English than the South Koreans or the Japanese, but where has this gotten them?

Professor Mazrui argues that cultural Westernization may not necessarily keep Africa from improved industrialization and

---

135 Mazrui, *Africa and Other Civilizations*, p. 258.
136 Ibid.

economic performance, but the key to economic development is "combining Western innovation with local authenticity."[137]

It is the same principle in every instance where a culture starts off locally and then comes to dominate others. With respect to religion, the issue can be explosive. However, piety should never have to hinge on blind imitation, whether of Arab or any other culture. Nor is there any need to substitute Western customs uncritically for Arab customs. What Muslims should be doing is learning and adapting to new circumstances. This, rather than cultural imitation, should be their guiding principle.

In time, a new synthesis will emerge from their selection of what is best in every culture with which they come into contact.

---

137   Mazrui, *Africa and Other Civilizations*, p. 259.

CONCLUSION

One Country,
Different Peoples

[When] the world is compelled to coin a new term to take account of increasingly widespread bigotry—it is a sad and troubling development. Such is the case with "Islamophobia" ... Since the September 11 attacks on the United States, many Muslims, particularly in the West, have found themselves the objects of suspicion, harassment and discrimination ... Too many people see Islam as a monolith and as intrinsically opposed to the West ... [The] caricature remains widespread and the gulf of ignorance is dangerously deep.

—**Kofi Annan**
Secretary General of the United Nations, speaking at UN conference, "Confronting Islamophobia: Education for Tolerance and Understanding" (December 7, 2004)

I began this book with a discussion of Samuel Huntington's theory of "a clash of civilizations" because it is so provocative, it has ignited a worldwide debate. Because it is also flawed and intellectually limiting, this debate has become open ended—subject to the vagaries of ongoing politics and holding out little promise of a conclusion. Huntington's views epitomize not merely the shortsightedness, but the *willful* shortsightedness that passes for wisdom about Islam in the West.

Belief in the looming danger of a clash of civilizations is just that: a *belief.* Promulgated by both Huntington and Bernard Lewis, it boasts a range of followers—from media pundits to government and political-party officials. To them, Islam is uniquely responsible for the problems of terrorism around the world and cultural dissonance in the heart of the West—the number one public enemy.

I followed this discussion with chapters purporting to describe the real problems associated with the Muslim presence in Europe and North America. After that I plotted what I judge is the best way out of the current predicament.

In hindsight, the stridency with which Islam has been debated by extremists on every side is a phenomenon that needs to be put in proper perspective. I am inclined to think that, aside from the acrimony and ignorance it has revealed, the encounters have had the net positive effect of provoking Muslims and people of other faiths to contemplate alternatives to the status quo.

Former Iranian president Muhammad Khatami's idea of a "dialogue of civilizations" was warmly received by the UN. It spurred the Spanish and Turkish prime ministers to advocate more forcefully for a more principled alignment of civilizations. This is one current of thinking that I hope will take root in international relations.

The second current, the one that interests me for the purpose of this book, consists of those Muslim intellectuals whose ideas have contributed to a growing consensus that any "clash of civilizations" would have multiple causes and, therefore, must be studied from various angles. Alone, difference of culture does not necessarily lead to clash. Indeed, from a historical perspective, culture has provided the perfect setting for countless positive exchanges among peoples (e.g., trade, knowledge, and so forth).

I find that the best solution for the Muslims of Europe and the West in general resides in a proper balance of identities, not the displacement of one identity to make room for the other. The first generation of Muslims in Western Europe lived out their lives in barracklike neighborhoods, separate from the national life buzzing around them. Nevertheless they survived and exert a collective *presence* of sorts. Thanks to their social isolation, they passed on their ethnic culture as best they could in the absence of any other. Some among their offspring have either abandoned their Islamic identity and assimilated fully into Swiss society or retreated behind illusory walls not unlike those their parents once faced.

Such a choice requires "either this way or that"—black or

white. I have tried to show that there is a third, more sustainable way. Based on Islam's most authentic sources, one can be both Muslim *and* Western. It is not necessary for every Swiss citizen to embrace it. It concerns Muslims, above all. But the other side too has to march forward, questioning this cultural assumption and overturning that. Will the twain ever meet? Will Muslims be able to merge the two identities?

There is a certain level at which they no doubt shall. One need only consider how many values are truly shared.

Tariq Ramadan is quoted by Hunter stating that "if there is to be a true and equal dialogue between Europeans and Muslims, Europe's universal values should enter into a dialogue with Islam's universal values."[138] Hunter concluded that this holds "the best hope of providing a bridge between Europe's absolute secularism and Muslims' attachment to their religious beliefs."[139]

For it to happen, though, society has to open itself enough to permit the active participation of everyone, with no exception. Unfortunately, the effect may not last very long if there are no qualified Muslim clerics, scholars, and intellectuals. Someone has to take the helm, but today leadership is sorely lacking in Switzerland and other countries with new Muslim populations.

Here is how I envisage the conscious process that can take us to a far more fruitful relationship:

1. Dialogue among Muslims and analysis of their situation in their Western countries

2. Development of representative leadership and a coherent collective position

3. Nurturing of Muslim communities locally and of organizations nationally

---

138   Hunter, *Reformist Voices of Islam*, p. 208.
139   Ibid., p. 264.

4. Development of universal standards for Muslims based on the fundamental principles of Islam

5. Institutional support for Muslims seeking spiritual support (*ijtihād* to interpreting and examining Islamic scriptures and focusing on sources such as *'urf*)

6. Empowerment to choose a multilayered identity and feel at home in Europe

7. Mobilization for full and active participation in European society

8. Adoption of the best in Swiss tradition that is consonant with Islam's highest principles

9. Discarding the hackneyed, outdated division between *dar al-Islam* (the abode of Islam) and *dar al-harb* (the abode of war)

10. More multicultural mosques where imams deliver their sermons in any of Switzerland's national languages

If the Qur'an declares that God seeks no difficulty for those who choose to worship him (5:6, 4:60), then Muslims should ask themselves: why all the burdens today?

Their burdens today are born of an internal conflict. Local customs continuously overlay the illusion of permanency upon *impermanent* features of Islamic tradition. Customs are an inescapable part of social life, and Islam is no exception. The difference is the sophistication with which Islamic tradition has negotiated the role of customs within a single faith. With or without religious scholars, every generation has to identify the fundamental principles of Islam without which local customs cannot be properly integrated.

Rather than reject 'urf wholesale and thus disembody Islam from its concrete expression in daily life, Western Muslims have to employ it as a key element in their effort to transcend their existing conflict of identity. At the same time Islam offers certain core principles without which it would make little sense to speak of Islam as a single religion. Therefore, Muslims should not be expected to renounce their faith just because someone happens to see only menace in Islam.

Muslims need to understand that Islam offers untold possibilities for practicing their faith across cultures and ethnicity. The object is not to sever ties with their ancestral lands. It is more significant than that. How the Muslims of Switzerland work 'urf into their lives will depend on their willingness to reflect critically and purposefully on the process of integration. The rewards cannot be overstated. Muslims will find common ground with fellow Swiss citizens on core issues that matter to all.

Clearly, this process will succeed only when all parties without exception embrace the revitalizing force of change. Switzerland is made up of a multiplicity of cultures, a diversity it should do its best to preserve, not degrade. Seeking common ground is not, and shouldn't be, about extirpating difference. Uniformity will not necessarily bring peace. What has to diminish is the tension. Out of diversity unity will emerge.

I am confident of this. The affinities of Muslims and non-Muslims are more pervasive than generally recognized. On the one hand, Islam accepts difference. On the other, Switzerland accepts the democratic protection of difference; its constitution has the potential of allowing all citizens to be part of the *ummah al-Swisriyyah* (Swiss community), so to speak.

But we all know that theory is one thing and practice another.

The guarantee of religious freedom as a human right thus includes the protection of individual faith and conscience and likewise the right to a public perception of this freedom. This includes a wealth of religious expressions such as worship, cultural activities, procession, but also ritual dances, songs, and ceremonies, provided they bring particular religious convictions. The same applies for buildings that serve as concrete expression of the individual and the common faith and that serve common events, such as churches, bell towers, mosques, minarets, synagogues, or temples of different types [*my translation*].[140]

Freedom of religion is meaningless if it cannot be guaranteed in practice. No minority, religious or otherwise, should see its rights suppressed in the interest of passing currents of public opinion, even when they are expressed through referenda.

Platform of reflexivity

This work reaffirms the importance of both parties to participate in dialogue. However, the best method for paving the way to meaningful dialogue is for each side to define the core principles they hold dearest and to see how they govern their respective identities. Switzerland has room to build a more inclusive federation based on constitutional law.

The following diagram summarizes what I have been arguing all along:

---

140   Wohlrab-Sahr/Tezcan, *Konfliktfeld Islam in Europa*, pp. 46–47.

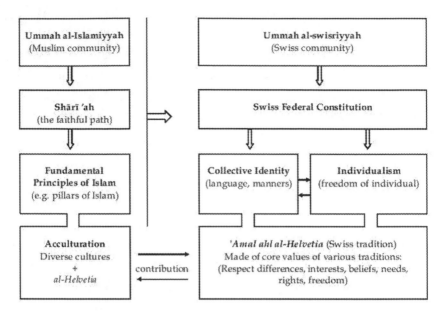

Ummah al-Islamiyyah (Muslim community)		Ummah al-swisriyyah (Swiss community)
Shārī'ah (the faithful path)	⟹	Swiss Federal Constitution
Fundamental Principles of Islam (e.g. pillars of Islam)		Collective Identity (language, manners) / Individualism (freedom of individual)
Acculturation Diverse cultures + al-Helvetia	⟶ contribution ⟵	'Amal ahl al-Helvetia (Swiss tradition) Made of core values of various traditions: (Respect differences, interests, beliefs, needs, rights, freedom)

Diagram 3 Acculturation process of Switzerland's Muslims

Although the left side relates to the Muslim community (first row), other religious or nonreligious groups may undergo a similar process of transformation, the end of which is bridge building across Swiss society.

The second row of the left side shows how Muslims may strive to remain faithful (Shārī'ah) to the Qur'an (the revelation of God), Sunnah (the way of the Prophet Muhammad), and *Usul al-fiqh* (the fundamental principles of Islamic law and jurisprudence). Shārī'ah does not equal cutting off the hands of thieves or stoning those who commit adultery. The Qur'an was revealed for the time and context of Prophet Muhammad. During that short period, the Prophet's Companions (*sahaba*) and earliest scholars read a scripture that, although sacred and divinely revealed, also contained guidance within a specific social environment.[141] Islam begins with the concrete; it does not impose burdens disproportional with reality.

---

141   Tariq Ramadan, *Radical Reform: Islamic Ethics and Liberation* (Oxford: Oxford University Press, 2009), p. 79.

There is no single Islamic culture. I have taken Arab customs as a model for arguing that no culture may be considered compatible with Islam to the exclusion of others. Just as they have been shaped by Islam, so the original Arab customs have pointed the way for all Muslims to practice their religion. Therefore, Shari'ah can only mean following the *path* of faith within, not without, the Swiss context.

The critical reasoning on which ijtihad, or personal reasoning, is based has enabled Muslims to face every challenge, and continues to do so. However, critical reasoning is possible even in the absence of qualified doctors of law, if at least common sense can combine with creativeness. The story of Mu'adh ibn Jabal, named by Prophet Muhammad as the judge of Yemen, is a case in point. Before leaving for his new post, the Prophet asked him, "Through what will you judge?" Mu'adh replied that he would judge through "the Book of God."

The Prophet then said, "And if you find nothing in the Book of God?"

"I shall judge according to the tradition [sunnah] of God's Messenger," said Muadh.

"And if you find nothing in the Messenger's tradition?"

"I shall not fail to make an effort [*ajtahidu*] to reach an opinion," Muadh said confidently.

Satisfied, the Prophet declared, "Praise be to God, who has guided His Messenger's messenger to what satisfies God's Messenger."

There is no substitute for understanding the fundamental texts and following the straight path. However, Muslims cannot truly remain faithful to God's Word revealed in the Qur'an and to the Sunnah by sticking to a single formula or solution for all time and place, with no regard to circumstance. The creative intelligence and simple common sense given them by God brings them closer to his purpose and the principles derived from it.[142]

The prospects for cultural plurality grow dimmer the longer that ethnicity (in the case of Muslims, old traditions that have evolved in their ancestral lands) enslaves people. When social groups or communities feel mistreated and unaccepted, they are much more likely to exhibit a slavish dependence on the behavioral and cultural consequences of their exclusion. If even the native Swiss find it difficult to participate fully in a newly adopted city or to make friends, imagine what it is like for non-natives.

The idea of collective identity may pose a direct challenge to Swiss policy makers who believe that everyone—migrants and native Swiss ethnicities—should feel comfortable and welcome. However, the challenge is for everyone to strive for the proper etiquette within the larger Swiss society—learning at least one of the national languages is but one example of such etiquette.

Differences will always separate people according to the interests, idiosyncrasies, needs, and rights they judge are properly theirs. They must be respected. People are entitled to join or belong to any religious community they want without being mistreated or threatened. As long as the Swiss People's Party (SVP) and their imitators insist on pursuing an agenda based on the politics of hate, viewing all *Ausländern* (foreigners) as criminals and blaming them for every problem, social transformation stands less chance of success.

There is a great need for a policy-making framework that actually works. In this vein, here are the highlights of what my book advocates:

- Encourage the population to accept and respect diversity.

---

142   Tariq Ramadan, *In the Footsteps of the Prophet: Lessons from the Life of Muhammad* (Oxford: Oxford University Press, 2007), pp. 199–200 and 2009:24.

- Work to help stop xenophobia.
- Create space for constructive dialogues with different religious groups.
- Develop a religious curriculum for Islam in Swiss universities to train clergypeople.
- Help turn the words of the constitution into deeds by walking the talk.

Teaming up for the Seven Goals

Why not assemble a group of experts to work together in mutual respect toward the following goals:

1. Correct inaccuracies in perceptions of Islam.

2. Establish continuous and constructive dialogue.

3. Make sure the voices of the younger generations are heard.

4. Transcend ethnicity, language, and group beliefs for the purpose of dialogue, without having to lose them.

5. Find the middle ground that bridges differences.

6. Explore the redefinition of the Swiss collective identity.

7. Empower Swiss society—at the local, regional, and national levels—to construct more conciliatory and productive approaches to social conflict.

The obstacles

Switzerland's Muslims are almost as heterogeneous as the Islamic world. This can present a serious obstacle to finding a recognized and competent leadership. I consider such leadership essential to the indigenization of Islam and the rise of a Euro-Muslim identity that incorporates the best features of both Islam and the host society. However, the internal dialogue among Muslims may prove rockier than one might anticipate, and the level of stress on this front could make dialogue between Muslims and non-Muslims less fruitful.

We have to be ready for the long haul. Radical views will always be part of each side. Extremism takes many forms. Sometimes it is religious (Islamists, fundamentalist Christians), sometimes ideological (far-right-wing politicians and their imitators).

Is faith a positive instrument?

Religion has the potential to either divide and destroy or unite and transform. Johan Galtung and Graeme MacQueen identify these "dual cultures" in all three Abrahamic faiths: "Culture of Peace" and "Culture of War."[143]

	Judaism	Christianity	Islam
Peace culture	And he shall judge among the nations—and they shall beat their swords into plowshares and their spears into pruning hooks: nation shall not lift up sword against nation, neither shall they learn war any more (Isaiah 2:4).	How blest are the peacemakers, God shall call them his sons (Matt. 5:9).	And whoever saves the life of a human being, it is as if he had saved all of mankind (Qur'an 5:32).

---

143   Johan Galtung and Graeme MacQueen, *Globalizing God: Religion, Spirituality and Peace* (Bergen: Kolofon Press, 2008), 63.

War culture	For in the cities within the boundaries of the Promised Land you are to save no one; destroy every living thing (Deut. 20:16–17).	Don't imagine that I came to bring peace to the earth. No, rather, a sword (Matt. 10:34).	Fight for the sake of God those that fight against you but do not attack them first (Qur'an 2:190).

The Qur'anic call for unity among the People of the Book is based on its recognition of a single uninterrupted prophetic tradition (42:13): *He hath ordained for you the same religion which He enjoined on Noah, and that which we have revealed to you [Muhammad], and that which we enjoined on Abraham and Moses and Jesus, saying: Establish religion, and be not divided therein.* Therefore, its admonition to keep conflict based over religious beliefs at a minimum is not hollow. It is essential to what it means to be Muslim.

Seeing how the history of Islam, Christianity, and Judaism are so closely intertwined, why not celebrate our common, Judeo-Christian-Islamic heritage? I do not mean that each historical-cultural identity within this heritage ought to be relinquished for a new culture for all. We are talking about a societal framework for coexistence made easier thanks to a long, shared history. At the same time, although we should not seek to efface specific cultural identities, at a societal level it is values, not specific articles of culture, that should be given precedence.

Switzerland may not end up a paradise of social tranquility. Wherever there are devout Muslims, Christians, and Jewish people, extreme fundamentalists of every stripe will prowl. There are even atheist and agnostic fundamentalists. It is all in the attitude. What level of respect are Switzerland's right-wing extremists ready to accord other human beings whose religious beliefs diverge from theirs?

I want to ask you, from another vantage point: what importance will these beliefs have when people of mainstream persuasions celebrate their differences?

There would be no need even to celebrate the weakening of extremism, because it would be irrelevant.

The main objective has to be to lift our fellow human beings from the trap of fear and hatred, to which people of goodwill anywhere risk falling victim. If they have been taught to hate, they can learn to love.

Switzerland is a collection of cultures and a work in progress, like any country on earth. Many "Swiss natives" trace their ancestries to the lands of Germany, France, Italy, Austria, and as far away as Scandinavia. It has not been a utopia, but whatever their presence has brought, they possess one of the most valuable experiences: coexistence. I am of the conviction that the native Swiss are so well placed that they can act as the midwife for a greater, richer, and better Switzerland. The country faces too many other challenges—poverty and equality of opportunity—to let cultural suspicion hobble public policy.

The stereotypes that Muslims and non-Muslims have formed about each other must be tackled head-on. So, let us be clear. Neither the native Swiss, be they Christian or atheist, nor Islam preaches the murder of innocents—terrorism. Islam does not condone female circumcision or honor killing. These are a part of different cultures, and they are growing moribund by the day. Almost all Swiss Muslims agree they have no place here.

The Swiss are an industrious people who, for generations, have been able to channel their talents and human resources productively. Surely there are mature minds in the country, perhaps well versed on the issues broached in this book, who can take the lead. Sadly it is not only Muslims who lack good leadership.

The bottom line

The first chapter of the Federal Constitution of the Swiss Confederation states, "All human beings are equal before the law" (Article 8), and "The freedom of religion and philosophy is guaranteed" (Article 15). Therefore, in principle, Jewish people, Christians, Buddhists, Muslims, and others have the right to practice their faiths.

The trouble is, how can a faith perceived as unfit for secular democratic values be accorded a place in Swiss society? How can Muslims be accommodated if "Islam" itself is intrinsically opposed to Western "liberal values"?

How we define a problem often determines the type of answer received—and whether or not there is an answer in the first place. Demonizing Islam predetermines what we envisage as being the right answer and the final solution it demands. I would venture to say that Europe has already visited this path once before, and the result has been catastrophic.

When the premises are false, then the reasoning is either weak or invalid. Therefore, one needs to revise them. In our case, the entire approach is at fault, and it is taking us nowhere.

Reform-minded Muslim scholars have done much to disprove the false view that Islam is inherently discordant with modernity and Western democratic values. When they or I insist that the Muslims of Europe have to be European, my words are well within both the pre-referendum Swiss Constitution and the teachings of the Qur'an.

You shall have your religion and I shall have my religion, teaches the Qur'an (109:6). *O mankind!* it reads, *We have created you male and a female; and we have made you into nations and tribes so that you may know one another* (49:13)—in other words, not so you can fight or use your differences to deny each other rights. One of Islam's core principles is that there is no compulsion in matters of religion. Muslims cannot force conversion upon non-Muslims, because *There shall be no coercion in religion* (Qur'an, 2:256). *The Truth is from your Lord; so let whoever wills, believe, and let whoever will, disbelieve* (18:29). But neither will they accept compulsion from others.

If the Swiss Federal Constitution and Holy Qur'an both promote equality and exhort people to recognize religious diversity, then the tensions between Muslims and non-Muslims must have other than "intrinsic" causes. Moreover, in the grand scheme of things these causes should not be intractable. We have a long history to prove it. The European Renaissance and Enlightenment owe a debt to Islam, as I have shown. Christians and Jewish people have worshipped freely in the lands of Islam while being brutally persecuted in Europe for *religious* reasons. And yet intercultural and even interreligious exchanges continued, because they are essential to human progress. The more interaction, the better people are able to figure out how to build a better, more stable world.

Therefore, our guiding principle in the heart of Europe should be "out of many, one." The politics of exclusion accomplishes little in comparison. It only entangles the interests of one party with another in unseemly ways, without freeing either one, and exacerbates the climate of insecurity. Extremists thrive even more on the resulting tensions without changing the nature of their solutions one iota. What they propose remains self-serving and sterile.

Extinguishing the fire

Blowing the smoke away would not help. If we want to stop it from spreading, we have to look beyond the smoke enveloping us. This is what I have tried to do through this book, but I also decided a while back that it is best to start with the community I know best.

I challenge the Muslims of Switzerland, just like those of the rest of Europe, to separate Islam from their ethnicity and to aim at re-creating the ummah from the universal principles of Islam in a new context.

I will never forget that incident where a group of fellow

Muslims openly accused me of being a spy and *kafir* (unbeliever), simply because I brought a poster to the mosque announcing a conference on *"Islam scharia im Wandel"* ("Islamic law in transition"). What provoked the heated exchange that took place was the German word *Wandel*, or "transition."

The memory has kept me going. I want never to betray my community. I do not want it to remain in the frigid cold of "exclusion politics," nor do I wish to push it over the edge of moral tolerance. But then, it is not even a question of trying to balance these two opposite poles, but a choice for a new, more inclusive world worthy of the twenty-first century. I hope that Switzerland and the Western world in general will take a leaf from reform-minded people with respect to peaceful coexistence. Awake.

Bibliography

Abdul Rauf, Feisal. *What's Right with Islam: A New Vision for Muslims and the West.* New York: Harper Collins, 2005.

Ahmad, Ahmad Atif. *Islam, Modernity, Violence, and Everyday Life.* New York: Palgrave Macmillan, 2009.

Al-Azmeh, Aziz. *Islam and Modernities.* 3rd ed. London: Verso, 2009.

Al-Djazairi, S. E. *The Golden Age and Decline of Islamic Civilization.* Manchester (UK): Bayt al-Hikma Press, 2006.

Al-Maaly, Khalid, Hg. *Die Arabische Welt: Zwischen Tradition und Moderne.* Heidelberg, Germany: Palmyra Verlag, 2004.

Arkoun, Mohammed. *Islam: To Reform or To Subvert?* London: Saqi Books, 2006.

ARTE (a European public-service cultural television channel). http://www.arte.tv/de/.

Baumann, Martin, and Stolz, Jörg. *Eine Schweiz – vielen Religionen: Risiken und Chancen des Zusammenlebens.* Bielefeld (Germany): Transcript Verlag, 2007.

Basler Zeitung, SVP möchte lieber „Maria Statt Scharia." Accessed October 23, 2010. http://schweizerkrieger.

wordpress.com/2009/02/16/maria-statt-scharia-ein-gelungenes -plakat/.

Berry, John W., Jean S. Phinney, David L. Sam, and Paul Vedder, eds. *Immigration Youth in Cultural Transition: Acculturation, Identity, and Adaptation Across National Contexts.* New Jersey: Lawrence Erlbaum, 2006.

Best, Ulrich, and Dirk Gebhardt. "Ghetto-Diskurse: Geographie der Stigmatisierung in Marseille und Berlin." In *Praxis Kultur- und Sozialgeographie* 24. Edited by Wilfried Heller, Potsdam: Universitätsverlag Potsdam, 2001. *Bundesamt für Statistik BFS* (Swiss Federal Statistical Office). Accessed August 23, 2010. http://www.bfs.admin.ch/bfs/ portal/ de/tools/search.simple.html.

Bundesversammlung—Das Schweizer Parliament. Accessed October 23, 2010. http://www.parlament.ch/d/ wahlenabstimmungen/volksabstimmungen/ volksab stimmungen -2009/abstimmung-2009-11-29/minarette/ seiten/default.aspx.

Chomsky, Noam. "The U.S. and Its Allies Will Do Anything to Prevent Democracy in the Arab World" in *Democracy Now!* Accessed May 21, 2011. http://www.democracy now. org/2011/5/11/noam_chomsky_the_us_and_its.

Daniel, Norman. *Islam and the West: The Making of an Image.* Oxford: Oxford University Press, 1993.

Esposito, John L., and Dalia Mogahed. *Who Speaks for Islam? What a Billion Muslims Really Think.* New York: Gallup, 2007.

Esposito, John L., and François Burgat. *Modernizing Islam: Religion in the Public Sphere in Europe and the Middle East.* New Jersey: Rutgers University Press, 2003.

Esposito, John L., and John O. Voll. *Makers of Contemporary Islam.* Oxford: Oxford University Press, 2001.

Euro-Islam.info (News and Analysis on Islam in Europe and North America). Accessed August 23, 2010. http://www. euro-islam.info/.

Fadil, Nadia. "Muslim Girls in Belgium: Individual Freedom through Religion?" *ISIM Newsletter* 13 (2003): 18–19. www. isim.nl.

Federal Administration Press Release. "Council Opposes Building Ban on Minarets: Opinion on the Popular Initiative Against the Construction of Minarets." August 27, 2008. Accessed October 29, 2010. http://www.ejpd. admin.ch/ejpd/en/home/ dokumentation/mi/2008/2008-08-27.html.

Fischer, Michael M. J. and Mehdi Abedi. *Debating Muslims: Cultural Dialogues in Postmodernity and Tradition.* Madison: University of Wisconsin Press, 1990.

Fox, Jonathan. "Two Civilizations and Ethnic Conflict: Islam and the West." *Journal of Peace Research* 38, no. 4 (2001): 459–72. http://www.jstor.org/.

Fox, Jonathan. "State Failure and the Clash of Civilizations: An Examination of the Magnitude and Extent of Domestic Civilisational Conflict from 1950 to 1996." *Australian Journal of Political Science* 38, no. 2 (2003): 195–213. http://www.jstor. org/.

Fukuyuma, Francis. *The End of History and the Last Man.* New York: Free Press, 1992.

Fukuyuma, Francis. *Islam and the West.* Oxford: Oxford University Press, 1993.

Fukuyuma, Francis. "The End of History?" *The National Interest* 16 (Summer 1989). Accessed October 24, 2010. http://www. wesjones.com/eoh.htm.

Fukayama, Francis. "The Permanent Online Archive for C-SPAN's Award-Winning Author Interview Program."

Booknotes.org. Accessed October 24, 2010. http://www. booknotes.org/Transcript/? ProgramID=1088.

Galtung, Johan. *50 Years: 100 Peace & Conflict Perspectives.* Bergen: Kolofon Press, 2008.

Galtung, Johan, and Graeme MacQueen. *Globalizing God: Religion, Spirituality and Peace.* Bergen: Kolofon Press, 2008.

Galtung, Johan. *A Theory of Peace: Overcoming Direct Violence.* Bergen: Kolofon Press, 2010.

Galtung, Johan. *A Theory of Development: Overcoming Structural Violence.* Bergen: Kolofon Press, 2010.

Gerholm, Tomas, and Yngve George Lithman, eds. *The New Islamic Presence in Western Europe.* London: Mansell, 1988.

Gianni, Matteo, unter Mitwirkung von Mallory Scheuwly Purdie, Stéphane Lathion, and Jenny Magali "Muslime in der Schweiz: Identitätsprofile, Erwartungen und Einstellungen." Eine Studie der Forschungsgruppe "Islam in der Schweiz GRIS" von Eidgenössische Kommissionsfragen (EKM), Zweite Auflage. Bern: Bundespublikation, 2010.

Gräf, Bettina, and Jakob Skovgaard-Petersen. *Global Mufti: the Phenomenon of Yūsuf al- Qaradāwi.* New York: Columbia University Press, 2009.

Gross, Adrea, Fredi Krebs, Martin Schaffner, and Martin Stohler, eds. *Von der Provokation zum Irrtum: Menschenrechte und Demokratie nach dem Minarett-Bauverbot.* St-Ursanne (Switzerland): Editions le Doubs, 2010.

Haley, Alex. *The Autobiography of Malcolm X.* New Jersey: Research & Education Association, 1996.

Halliday, Fred. *Islam & the Myth of Confrontation.* New York: I. B. Tauris, 1996.

Harrison, Lawrence E., and Samuel P. Huntington. *Culture Matters: How Values Shape Human Progress.* New York: Basic Books, 2000.

Herzog, Roman. *Wider den kampf der kulturen: Eine Friedenstrategie für das 21. Jahrhundert.* Translated by Theo Sommer. Frankfurt a.M: S. Fischer. Original version: *Preventing the Clash of Civilizations.* New York: St. Martin, 1999.

Jochen Hippler, "The Islamic Threat and Western Foreign Policy,"in *The next threat: Western perceptions of Islam,* edited by Jochen Hippler and Andrea Lueg; translated by Laila Friese (London: Pluto Press, 1995), p. 116-153.

Huda, Qamar-ul. *Crescent and Dove: Peace and Conflict Resolution in Islam.* Washington, DC: United States Institute of Peace Press, 2010.

Hunter, Shireen T., ed. *Reformist Voices of Islam: Mediating Islam and Modernity.* New York: M. E. Sharpe, 2009.

Hunter, Shireen T. *The Future of Islam and the West: Clash of Civilizations or Peaceful Coexistence?* Westport (CT): Praeger, 1998.

Huntington, Samuel P. "The Clash of Civilizations?" *Foreign Affairs* 72, no. 3 (1993): 22–49.

Huntington, Samuel P. *The Clash of Civilizations and the Remaking of World Order.* London: Free Press, 2002.

Huntington, Samuel P. "If Not Civilizations, What?" *Foreign Affairs* 72, no. 4 (1993): 186–94.

Izzi Dien, Mawil. *Islamic Law: From Historical Foundations to Contemporary Practice.* Edinburg: Edinburgh University Press, 2004.

Islam, Shada. "Beyond Minarets: Europe's Growing Problem with Islam: Can One Be Both European and Muslim?" *YaleGlobal* (2020). Accessed October 24, 2010. http://

yaleglobal.yale.edu/content/ beyond-minarets-europes-growing-problem.

Kamali, Mohammad Hashim. *Principles of Islamic Jurisprudence*. 3rd ed. Cambridge: Islamic Texts Society, 2003.

Kettani, Houssein. "2010 World Muslim Population." *Proceedings of the 8th Hawaii International Conference on Arts and Humanities*, Honolulu (2010): 1–61. Accessed August 23, 2010. http://www.pupr.edu/hkettani/papers/HICAH2010. pdf.

Khatami, Muhammad. "Dialogue Among Civilizations." UNESCO, 2000. Accessed May 24, 2010. http://www. unesco.org/dialogue/en/khatami.htm.

Kirbassov, Galymzhan. "Has 'the Clash of Civilizations' Found Empirical Support?" *The Fountain* 14, no. 56 (2006). Accessed May 5, 2010. http://www.fountainmagazine. com/ article.php? ARTICLEID=783.

Kochler, Hans. "The 'Clash of Civilizations': Perception and Reality in the Context of Globalization and International Power Politics." Lecture on *Globalization and a Dialogue Between Civilizations*, Tsereteli Institute of Oriental Studies (Georgian Academy of Sciences), Tbilisi, Georgia 2004.

Küpper, Beate. "Da sind derzeit all Schleusen offen." *taz.de*. Accessed January 29, 2010. http://www.taz.de/1/leben/ alltag/artikel/1/da-sind-derzeit-alle-schleusen-offen/.

Lapidus, Ira M. *A History of Islamic Societies*. Cambridge: Cambridge University Press, 1991.

Lexis-Nexis (database for magazines and newspapers): http:// lexisnexis.ch/.

Lewis, Bernard. *From Babel to Dragomans: Interpreting the Middle East*. London: Phoenix, 2005.

Lewis, Bernard. "The Roots of Muslim Rage." *The Atlantic Monthly* 266, no. 3 (1990): 47–60. Accessed May 24, 2010. http://www.theatlantic.com/magazine/archive/1990/09/the-roots-of-muslim-rage/4643/.

Loewenstein, Antony. "Hatred and Fear of Islam in Switzerland Is Connected to Previous Hatreds." (March 21, 2010). Accessed October 29, 2010. http://antonyloewenstein.com/2010/03/21/ hatred-and-fear-of-islam-in-switzerland-is-connected-to-previous-hatreds/.

Mazrui, Ali A. *Africanity Redefined*. Edited by Ricardo Rene Laremont and Tracia Leacock Seghatolislami. Asmara, Eritrea: Africa World Press, 2002.

Mazrui, Ali Al Amin. *Africa and Other Civilizations: Conquest and Counter-Conquest*. Edited by Ricardo Rene Laremont and Fouad Kalouche. Asmara, Eritrea: Africa World Press, 2002.

Mazrui, Ali A. "Western Values and The Satanic Verses." In *Debating the African Condition: Ali Mazrui and His Critics*. Edited by Alamin M. Mazrui and Willy M. Mutunga, vol. 1, 145–95. Asmara, Eritrea: Africa World Press, 2004.

Mazrui, Ali A. *Islam: Between Globalization and Counterterrorism*. Asmara, Eritrea: Africa World Press, 2006.

Michael Lüder, Hrsg. *Der Islam im Aufbruch? Perspectiven der arabischen Welt*. Serie Piper Band 1569. München: Piper, 1992.

Mottahedeh, Roy P. "The Clash of Civilizations: An Islamicist's Critique." *Harvard Middle Eastern and Islamic Review* 2, no. 2 (1995).

Müller, Wolfgang W. *Christentum und Islam: Plädoyer für den Dialog*. Zürich: Theologischer Verlag Zürich, 2009.

Nasr, Seyyed Hossein. *The Essential*. Edited by William C. Chittick. Indiana: World Wisdom, 2007.

Norris, Pippa, and Ronald Inglehart. "Islam & the West: Testing the 'Clash of Civilizations' Thesis." *John F. Kennedy School of Government Research Working Paper Series*, No. RWP02-015. Cambridge, MA: Harvard University, 2002.

Obama, Barack Hussein. "Text: Obama Speech in Cairo" in *New York Times*. Accessed October 24, 2010. http://www.nytimes.com/2009/06/04/us/politics/04obama.text. html.

Office for National Statistics. Bradford, UK, 2001 Census. Accessed August 23, 2010. http://www.statistics.gov.uk/census2001/profiles/00cx.asp.

Padilla, Amado M. "The Role of Cultural Awareness and Ethnic Loyalty in Acculturation." *Acculturation: Theory, Models and Some New Findings*. Boulder: Westview Press, 1980.

Pahud De Mortages, René, and Erwin Tanner, Hrsg. *Muslime und schweizerische Rechtsordnung / Les musulmans et l'ordre juridique suisse*. Freiburger Veröffentlichungen zum Religionsrecht (FVRR), Bd. 13. Freiburg: Schulthess, 2002.

Pauly, Robert J. *Islam in Europe: Integration or Marginalization?* Aldershot, Hants: Ashgate, 2004.

Puddington, Arch. "Freedom of Expression after the 'Cartoon Wars.'" *Freedom House*. Accessed August 23, 2010. http://www.freedomhouse.org/uploads/fop/ FOP2006 cartoonessay.pdf.

Rahman, Fazlur. *Revival and Reform in Islam. A Study of Islamic Fundamentalism*. Edited by Ebrahim Moosa. Oxford: Oneworld, 2003.

Ramadan, Tariq. "Europeanization of Islam or Islamization of Europe?" In *Islam, Europe's Second Religion*. Edited by Shireen T. Hunter. Westport, CT: Praeger, 2002.

Ramdan, Tariq. *To Be a European Muslim*. Leicester, UK: Islamic Foundation, 2002.

Ramadan, Tariq. *Islam, the West and the Challenges of Modernity.* Leicester, UK: Islamic Foundation, 2004.

Ramdan, Tariq. *Western Muslims and the Future of Islam.* Oxford: Oxford University Press, 2005.

Ramdan, Tariq. *In the Footsteps of the Prophet: Lessons from the Life of Muhammad.* Oxford: Oxford University Press, 2007.

Ramdan, Tariq. *Radical Reform: Islamic Ethics and Liberation.* Oxford: Oxford University Press, 2009.

Ramdan, Tariq. *What I Believe.* Oxford: Oxford University Press, 2010.

Rauf, Feisal Abdul. *What's Right with Islam: A New Vision for Muslims and the West.* New York: HarperOne, 2005.

Rosen, Lawrence. *The Culture of Islam: Changing Aspects of Contemporary Muslim Life.* Chicago: University of Chicago Press, 2004.

Roy, Olivier. *Globalised Islam: The Search of a New Ummah.* London: Hurst & Company, 2004.

Rushdie, Salman. *The Satanic Verses.* New York: Viking Press, 1988.

Said, Edward W. "The Clash of Ignorance." *The Nation.* Accessed May 24, 2010. http://www.thenation.com/ doc/20011022/ said.

Schaffroth, Thomas. "Die Ruhe zwischen den Rosenstöcken." *Die Wochenzeitung WOZ*, 19 (April 2007). Accessed August 23, 2010. http://www.woz.ch/artikel/inhalt/2007/ nr16/ International/15097.html.

Schulze, Reinhard. "Islam und Herrschaft: Zur politischen Instrumentalisierung einer Religion." *Der Islam im Aufbruch? Perspektiven der arabischen Welt.* Edited by Michael Lüder. München: Piper, 1993.

Schweizer Fernsehen (Swiss Television: SF): http://www.sf.tv/.

Smith, Jane I. "Islam and Christendom: Historical, Cultural and Religious Interaction from the Seventh to the Fifteenth Centuries." *The Oxford History of Islam*. Edited by John L. Esposito, 317–27. Oxford: Oxford University Press, 1999.

Salam, Soraya. "Muslim Women Who Cover in America" 2010 Cable *News Network* (CNN). Accessed August 23, 2010. http://religion.blogs.cnn.com/2010/08/23/muslim-women-who-wear-the-hijab-and-niqabexplain-their-choice/?hpt=C2.

Statistisches Jahrbuch der Stadt Bern. Berichtsjahr 2008. Accessed August 23, 2010. http://www.bern.ch/leben_in_bern/stadt/statistik/publikationen/jahrbuch/jahrbuch08i.pdf/view?searchterm=statistik.

Stüssi, Marcel. "Banning of Minarets: Addressing the Validity of a Controversial Swiss Popular Initiative." *Religion and Human Rights* 3 (2008): 135–53. Brill: Nijhoff.

Swissworlg.org. "History—Women." Accessed October 29, 2010. http://www.swiss world.org/en/history/the_20th_century /women/.

Sztompka, Piotr. *The Sociology of Social Change*. Oxford: Blackwell, 1994.

Tibi, Bassam. *Islam and Cultural Accommodation of Social Change*. Translated by Clare Krojzi. San Francisco: Westview Press, 1990.

Tibi, Bassam. *Euro-Islam: Die Lösung eines Zivilisationskonflikts*. Darmstadt: Primus Verlag, 2009.

Tibi, Bassam. "Europeanisation, Not Islamisation." *signandsight. com* (March 22, 2007). Accessed October 24, 2010. http://www.signandsight.com/features/1258.html.

Tiesler, Nina Clara. "Muslime in Europa: Religion und Identitätspolitiken unter veränderten gesellschaftlichen Verhältnissen." *Politik & Kultur* (Band 8). Berlin: LIT Verlag, 2006.

Tietze, Nikola. "Formen der Religiosität Junger Männlicher Muslime in Deutschland und Frankreich." *Islam in Sicht: Der Auftritt von Muslimen im öffentlichen Raum.* Edited by Nilüfer Göle and Ludwig Ammann. Bielefeld: Transcript Verlag, 2004.

Tranchet, Nancy, and Dianna Rienstra, eds. "Islam and the West: Annual Report on the State of Dialogue." *World Economic Forum*, Geneva, 2008, pp 1-156.

Turner, Bryan S. *Religion and Social Theory.* 2nd ed. London: Sage, 1994.

United Nations. "Dialogue Among Civilizations." United Nations Year of Dialogue Among Civilizations 2001. Accessed May 24, 2010. http://www.un.org/Dialogue/.

University of Bern. Invitation to lecture and panel discussion on Islamic family law. Accessed October 23, 2010. https://listserv.unibe.ch/pipermail/fachschaftislam/2006-January/000017.html.

University of Bern. Poster of public lecture on *"Muslimisches Familienrecht im Wandel."* Accessed October 23, 2010. https://listserv.unibe.ch/pipermail/fachschaftislam/attachments/20060122/2d397943/Einladung2-0001.pdf.

Vertovec, Steven, and Alisdair Rogers, eds. *Muslim European Youth: Reproducing Ethnicity, Religion, Culture.* Aldershot: Ashgate, 1998.

Voll, John O. "Conclusion: Asian Islam at a Crossroads." In *Asian Islam in the 21st Century.* Edited by John L. Esposito, John O. Voll, and Osman Bakar, 261–289. Oxford: Oxford University Press, 2008.

Watt, W. Montgomery. *Islam and the Integration of Society*. The International Library of Sociology, The Sociology of Religion, vol. 2. London: Rutledge, 1998.

Weber, Max. *The Protestant Ethic and the Spirit of Capitalism: with Other Writings on the Rise of the West*. Translated by Stephen Kalberg. 4th ed. Oxford: Oxford University Press, 2009.

Weber, Max. *Max Weber & Islam*. Edited by Toby E. Huff and Wolfgang Schluchter. New Brunswick: Transaction, 1999.

Willerstein, Immanuel. "Islam, the West, and the World." *Journal of Islamic Studies* 10, no. 2 (1999): 109–125. Oxford: Oxford University Press.

Wohlrab-Sahr, Monika, and Levent Tezcan, Hrsg. *Konfliktfeld Islam in Europa*. Soziale Welt, Sonderband 17. Baden-Baden: Nomos, 2007.

World Factbook. "Country Comparison on Life Expectancy at Birth." Accessed October 2, 2010. https://www.cia.gov/library/publications/the-world-factbook/rankorder/2102rank.html.